'When I were a

DARWEN
BOLTON

by Arthur Clayborough

Published by Jubilee Tower Enterprises,

Trondheim, 2023

ISBN 9798389245716

Jubilee Tower Enterprises assert

their rights to this work, no part may

be reproduced without permission.

When I were a Lad

by Arthur Clayborough

(Note to self: Bring old prewar Darwen back to life..).

Preface

We *were* poor at our house, but we could afford both a father and a mother, so that was all right. When I decided to be born, I was looking for responsible, selfless parents with warm hearts and a sense of humour.

I got two of them, and beyond that it didn't really matter if bath night was in front of the fire in a big zinc tub with a hole in the bottom plugged (not very well) with plasticine, or if I had to sit now and then in an outside lavatory with a big *Ever Ready* lamp hanging on a nail at the back of the door over a bunch of old *Radio Times*, or have my "kneelength boy's knickers" bought with clothing club cheques.

I had it made, all set for a glorious childhood, and I got one.

Contents

Preface	5
Untitled 1	7
Gating Up	8
Untitled 2	12
Us Mother (not 'Our Mam')	13
Les Doigts	18
Untitled 3	23
Scouting for Boys	25
Gravy Eyes	36
Owd Corran, Owd Danny	44
Fon	51
Why My Dad would only sit on the End Seat on the Back Row at the Pictures	52
My Musical Education	62
Going to Blackpoo'	68
My Bike George	87
Picknicking	91
The Landmine	101
The Chip Butty	107
Untitled 4	113
Algy and Tusker (and Icky)	114
Feighting	121
'Vote, vote, vote, fer 'erbert Samuel.'	133
The Boy With a Book	137
Kesmus	148
Wasting a Cephos	156
A Good Cath'o'licking	162
Scruffy Flower	171

The Olympia Entry	174
Untitled 5	178
Following Girls	179
He who knows nothing	191
Smoking	192
The Tower; A Poem in Blank Verse	195
The Raff	203
Untitled 6	208
And all the Rest	209
The Escalator	218
Alleyball	219

Untitled 1

When little Cortez discovered Holt's meadow
behind the nurse's home: and with his head
full of rose-names, planted his pigeon toes
among the brushwood in the burdock bed,
legs polished by the quiet to plastic steel:
that morning he had put out sugar for a fly
and his bottomless pockets had been sewn up at last.
He had outgrown almost nothing. In his eye
clear and uncataracted, the broken earth
proffered its rubbish like a sacred birth.
Up on the wall were glittering bits of glass
and dandelions shouted yellow songs.
Dock leaves grew rhubarb-big, manured with urine,
and the insect world went at it hammer and tongs.
The spider's riggish foot touched the cannibal web,
the shagged-out drone died on his honeymoon,
some gullible butterflies probed the sour flowers
with clockwork springs: and the fingers moved to noon.

Gating Up

My Dad used to start work at half-past six every working day (he worked a hundred hours a week) and that meant getting up in the dark at some unearthly time. At Blackpool he could have stayed in bed all day, but his body used to get him up at the same time as it did all the rest of the year, and he would go out on to the prom in the early morning cold and wait with the other "labourers" as they were called for a coffee stall to open. There would be a whole crowd of them, all pretending they had got up for a breath of "ozone".

Dad always lit the fire before he went out to join the other dark shapes trudging and stumbling across the Top, and he always did it the same way, though it was only now and then on Sundays that I got to watch him. He used a kind of home-made double-edged axe blade on a short, stout handle to split two- or three-inch-thick plates of wood into sticks, holding the wood upright with one hand and chopping like lightning with the other, within half-an-inch of his big fingers. I think it was a matter of pride with him to chop as fast as possible, like a a chef cutting up a carrot or a gambler shuffling cards. My mother hated to watch him, and when she was there the same dialogue always took place.

"Ee, Harry, do mind your fingers!"

"Ay, shurrup."

The grate had to be cleaned out first, then twists of *News Chronicle* or *Empire News* or *Darwen Advertiser* were laid down and covered with a little tent of sticks. The paper was lit and then the fireplace was blocked with the flat, blackened "blower", a sheet of metal with a handle in the middle.

There were blowerless people who lived dangerously, sticking a poker down the front of the grate, and spreading a sheet of newspaper over it. (Sooner or later a great brown patch would spread across the paper and then it would burst into flame.)

But Dad always used the blower, even when, later, it had big holes in it. I don't think we ever threw anything away, and I still don't. I can't.

You could hear the roar as the paper blazed up in the underdraught and the sticks began to crackle. The noise had a promise of warmth in it in the stone-flagged house (the living room was always called "the house"), and on the few days when we were downstairs when Dad lit the fire, usually at weekends, we used to creep nearer in our pyjamas and nightdresses and stick out our bare feet towards the sound. But then the blower had to be taken away to pile on largish pieces of coal ("cobs" or "best nuts" not "slack"), and the crackling firewood would send out showers of sparks ("Look up, now, get out't way ") through the old wire fireguard and out on the hearthrug.

There was a momentary glow of heat from the blazing wood, and then the blower was replaced, and we were in the cold again.

" It'll soon gate up," Dad would tell us, and we would sit there listening to the dull boom behind the blower until it was roaring for freedom behind the bars of the grate and the fireguard.

"All right, get back a bit!"

He would take the blower away and the heat would hit us as we moved our stools back. But then we would sit there getting our shins and our faces mottled with the heat, looking into the red coals until they had to be covered with "slack" - coarse coal dust and thick grey smoke spiralled up the chimney.

It was time to get dressed and have our breakfast, not always in that order.

The fireguard was a buckled old thing. There was a long wire at the back with a hook on it to keep it fastened to the grate. It came into a lot of my games, and I could stick lead soldiers and things like that in the wire lozenges, just as long as they weren't flammable. Sometimes they would fall inside the fire guard and the "fender" and have to be winkled out again with the poker.

On Friday nights I used to scrounge tuppence from Dad and run down Spring Gardens in the pitch dark to Mr.Kay's for a *Rover* or a *Wizard*. When I got back, I would lie full length on the rag rug (we had to turn it back away from the fire at bedtime) reading about *The Black Sapper* or *The Wolf of Kabul* and getting under the feet, especially when my mother was lowering and raising the rack. The rack hung down from two pulleys in the ceiling, and the washing hung down from the rack. If you stood in front of the fire warming your backside when mother had done a big washing, you were looking straight into a Nancy Jepson dress or a pair of overalls or a big, wet sheet, covered with yellowed patches. Sometimes you were even standing under or in between wet towels and sheets. They had been through the rollers on the mighty cast-iron squeezers in the kitchen, but they could still drip on your head or your comic.

Every so often Dad used to get down on the hearthrug to mend our shoes. His tackle was kept in an old black wooden box with a brass hook and eye at the front. He used a knife that had been sharpened so much that only half the blade was left. The shoe he was mending would be put on a black iron last with three legs, two ending in different sized feet and one in a heel. He used good, thick leather from old belting - in those days factory lathes were run from great belts -, shaped to size, professionally thinned out to the edges (Dad's brother was a cobbler) and nailed on with tiny brass nails.

I used to have to go to the ironmongers in the Market Hall and ask for mysteriously named things like "half an ounce of five-eighths brass rivets", "two 'tatchin'- ends" and a "heel-ball". Dad would put a dozen tiny brass nails in his mouth and hammer them one at a time into a groove in the new sole or heel. Heels were built up from two layers of belting, and any gaps were filled with melted heel-ball (whatever that was). He did a marvellous repair job, even if you did get the odd brass rivet sticking in your foot sole.

I used to watch everything he did, and I fondly imagine (probably wrongly) that I could mend a pair of shoes myself, if necessary, though I've never actually tried. I loved my Dad, sitting there in his old collarless union shirt and threadbare "weskit" after a fourteen-hours day shifting heavy machinery about, mending our shoes in front of the fire with a mouthful of "five-eighths brass rivets", though perhaps I didn't appreciate him as much as he deserved. But I was only a little boy, and it wouldn't have been possible anyway.

Untitled 2

A robust dream, and filled with coloured wind

blown sausage-wise with stars and unseen seas;

the streets hung down for us, before we sinned

and found our nutshells cells of little ease.

Chattering drainpipes, cobbles laced with glass,

toffee-hammer tomahawks,

butterflies exploding from the grass

and beetles clambering in the brushwood stalks:

One chair, one face, one hand, one spoon, one food,

the snottiest nose was not denied;

the world was richer then than we were rude

until we woke to find that we had died.

What was it made our happy-hunting-ground

a hell of shattered boards and rusty tins?

With all the talk, has anybody found

where innocence ends and ignorance begins?

Us Mother (not 'Our Mam')

We used to threaten one another with "I'll tell *us Dad*" but "I'll tell *us Mother*." I can't say whether that was just in our family..Perhaps it was because my Dad talked broad and my mother didn't, or at any rate tried not to. Her sisters called her "Our Edie". She wasn't a Darrener. She came from Radcliffe and was born in Little Lever, which to us was foreign parts where people talked different, a bit like Australia today, perhaps.

I never knew any of my grandparents. They died on the young side, and no wonder. My grandfather David John Mitchell was a miner, and my grandmother, Lizzie Field, came from Rochdale. My mother loved telling us stories, some true, some made up. She told me how when she was a little girl, she used to write an endless story about somebody called *Gipsy Fergundy*, and as she had nothing to write on, she went round collecting handbills from under people's door knockers and writing on the backs. I don't suppose it had as much as punch as *Martha Strang, Murderess* in *The Miracle,* though.

Us mother was very superstitious. She used to tell fortunes with cards, like: "There's a dark man with money coming into your life soon" (He never came into ours, not with money at any rate) and with tea-leaves. You had to drink the tea, turn the cup upside down and turn it round three times. Once when my mother was telling a neighbour's fortune, I pinched a teacup and shaped the leaves in it with a spoon into a little man and a number three. Her mouth dropped open until she looked at my face, and told me to get on with you, you cheeky little b*gger.

Flakes of soot fluttering on the bars at the front of the fire were "strangers" and meant that one would be turning up soon. I seem to remember faking a really big "stranger" for her, flapping on the grate in front of the fire- she saw through that - but the only big strangers I can remember actually turning up were Teresa's boyfriends. Some of them were pretty strange, too, like a big Canadian paratrooper called Prosper Willems who had broken his back, (he said he 'forgot his parachute'). The day he got out of hospital he drank fourteen light ales and went swimming, so I overheard. I also overheard Teresa telling our mother that he lived on a ranch out on the Canadian prairie with his dad and a couple of brothers, and all they said to one another was good morning and good night. That put her off a bit. Then he told her "If you stand on the stoop at the front of the farmhouse, Terry, what do you see? ... *Nothing, for miles!*"

I think that put the tin hat on it, and I was sorry because it meant that I wouldn't get to go riding across the Canadian prairie like Solo Solomon in the *Wizard* on my horse *Gasbag*. I still have that pleasure to come, but nowadays we are both getting a bit long in the tooth.

Getting back to mother's superstitions, dropping a knife or a fork meant somebody was coming. I think a knife meant a man, and a fork a woman, or the other way round. I don't know what you had to drop to make Uncle Harold turn up, as he did now and then. When old Uncle Evan, one of my mother's favourites, turned up from the other side of Bolton, sometimes wet through, he always looked as though somebody had dropped *him* into something.

His wife Auntie Polly, a neat, tidy little woman herself, tried to keep him neat and tidy too but it was hopeless. If he got an overcoat he popped it, probably to get pub money. I expect that was where his false teeth went. I remember once telling him, don't ask me why, that my pal Alan's dad, who was a chauffeur (posh by our standards) had put his cufflinks in exactly the same place on the corner of the fireplace every night for twenty years. Uncle Evan's comment was "He morn'd be gradely reet".

Mother's fortune-telling from people's dreams, their tea-leaves and cards were forbidden by the penny catechism we used to chorus in school:

"The Church forbids trusting to dreams, omens, fortune-telling and suchlike fooleries". I didn't know what *omens* were except that they must have been a bit like *amens* (I didn't know what they were either) but we liked shouting the "suchlike fooleries" bit. That had a real ring to it.

The penny catechism was one of the schoolbooks we used most, at Saint Joseph's. I can hear us now shouting the questions and answers. Usually, we hadn't the slightest idea what any of it meant, like "For what ends is the sacrifice of the Mass offered?" Answer: "The sacrifice of the Mass is offered for four ends..." I'm still a bit puzzled about those four ends.

And we chorused: "The Church has always forbidden mixed marriages, and considers them unlawful and pernicious...", and we shouted in blissful ignorance that we mustn't "marry within certain degrees of kindred, or solomonise marriages at the forbidden times", but nobody ever bothered to explain why, or what Solomon had to do with it. Our mother told me that when she was at school, she thought God's name was Harold. ("Harold be thy name"). She didn't get to go to school much because she had to look after her little sisters. She was proud of how young she was when she "passed for half-time and full- time". If you were clever then, they kicked you out. By the time I got to school, they had changed things. I wasn't clever enough to be kicked out.

In the infant school, the ingenious Miss Sefton taught us us our letters, chorussing them from the blackboard: For "E" , we cupped a hand to an ear and shouted a couple of dozen times: *"Deaf man, "Eh?", Deaf man "Eh?".* For "C", we shouted *"Cuh" wiv its mouf open, "Cuh" wiv its mouf open!".* When I sat under the table at home shouting my lessons, Mother thought I had finally gone funny, or at any rate, funnier, and wondered whether to call Nurse Worth, who looked a bit like *Sunny Jim* on the *Force* cornflakes packet. I once threw a handful of marbles at her.

One of my mother's favourite expressions was "as silly as a boat horse", but I couldn't see why boat horses were any sillier than other horses, neither could I tell you whether my mother was ever pretty or not. I once saw a younger photo of her with other girl munitions workers during the Great War (as we used to call it until another one came along), and she didn't look so bad ; but ordinary kids don't know (or bother) whether their parents are handsome or beautiful or not. Unless they are film stars, I suppose.

Mine weren't, though I thought my Dad looked a bit like his favourite actor, 'Owd Dosh Garnit' (Gabby Hayes) in his old union shirt. My mother's sisters thought he looked like, what's-he -called, that there French actor, *John Gabbang* were it? And (once, when they made him wear a hat for a wedding) they said he looked like *Trencer Spacey*.

I remember my mother's amazement when she found out (in her sixties) that she was only five feet three. ("Is that all I am? *Five foot three*? Ee, for goodness' sakes, I thought I were a lot taller than that!") It took her a bit to get over the shock. But she wore those toe-crushing shoes with highish heels which probably gave her a couple of inches extra, and at least during the war she wore a black hat with a sort of high crown which we called "the U-Boat" because Dad said she looked like a bl...y U-Boat commander in it. And she did have a nice straight Mitchell nose, not like the one *I* got from us Dad. Right on the front row, I was, when noses were handed out. But she was your mother, right? What did you care what she looked like? She was the biggest thing in your life while you were growing up, but you just took her for granted, like your own arms and legs.

I don't anymore, though.

Les Doigts

I suppose I was about eight, because I was in Owd Corran's class at the council school when I came across these little adverts in papers like John Bull or The Empire News for "Pelmanism".

I still don't know what Pelmanism was (or is) but I remember two things about the adverts, and they must have been quite dramatic to catch the attention of a rather dreamy eight-year-old.

First, there was a picture of a man being throttled with a striped tie, and some comment like ARE YOU STRANGLED BY YOUR OLD SCHOOL TIE?

Somewhere I've heard it said that there are two kinds of people strangled by the old school tie, those who have one and those who haven't, but whether that was the Pelman message or not, I can't remember.

Second, and more important for me, was the offer of a free French lesson, with the comment, A MAN WHO KNOWS TWO LANGUAGES IS TWICE AS GOOD AS THE MAN WHO ONLY KNOWS ONE.

There was an attached coupon which I filled out and sent in - I expect my mother posted it for me. A week or so later, a little white booklet arrived addressed to Arthur Clayborough Esquire.

It was illustrated with little pictures. The one I remember best was an open hand with the word " main" written underneath, and the queer words "doigts" and "ongles" written over the fingers. There was a leg with "jambe" written underneath, and a bit higher up, "genou".

I sat on a park bench near the duck pond puzzling it all out, rather like the princess learning English in *Henry the Fifth* ("de bilbow, de nick, de sin"), though, unlike me, she had somebody to help her.

I did once ask my Dad (but only once) about French. After all, he had been in France, in places with strange names like *Wipers* and *Dicky Bush*.

"Did you learn any French, Dad?" I asked.

"Well... Ah don't know." He looked a bit guilty for some reason.

" "Napoo", "Alley tootsweet". That's about the lot."

"What's "Napoo", Dad?"

"Well, it meant, like, "We haven't got nowt.""

"All that?"

"Aye."

"An' that..."tootsweet". What did that mean?"

"Aye, well, it meant, like, " Bugger off!"

(Mother: "That'll do, Harry! he's only a little lad.")

Perhaps there were hints to pronunciation ("lay dwa" and so on) in the free lesson. It seems likely. But as I had no idea that different languages were pronounced differently, they wouldn't have been much use to me in any case.

At the end of the brochure, I came across something I felt I could get my teeth into, numbers from 1 to 10 with the French names underneath. I said them aloud until I had got them by heart: *un, dukes, troyz, quarter, sink, six, sept, hewit, newf, dicks.*

After a certain amount of mental wrestling, I could even continue the weird list as far as 20:

onz, dooze, trys, quatters, quins, seas, dicks-sept, dicks-hewit, dicks-newf, vingt.

I recited them over and over all the way across the Tippings.

Together with the little booklet, came a list of prices for the following lessons and the full course. I forget what they were, except that they were in guineas. I expect they were reasonable enough. Some days later, the little booklet came again with another list of prices, and a week later I got yet another set, before somebody decided that Arthur Clayborough Esquire was as short of brass as they were, and a dead loss.

It can't have been more than a few weeks later when for some reason Owd Corran got on to France, and with a mixture of pride and embarrassment on my face, I put my hand up.

"Please sir, I can count up to ten in French."

Billy Stevenson, Frank Condon, Basil O'Gorman, Leonard Walmsley and the rest listened with envy and scepticism on their faces.

"Go on, then," said Owd Corran.

"Un dukes troyz quarter sink six sept hewit newf dicks," I reeled off, proud, but modest with it.

In the silence that fell, you could hear the classroom mouse pulling drinking straws for its nest out of the wastepaper basket.

Then Owd Corran said firmly,

"No. It's all wrong."

I stared at him, bewildered. Was The Pelman Institute just a fraud?

There was an underswell of giggling.

"Please sir, I read it in like a little book I sent up for."

"Yes, yes, yes, but you've got it all wrong. It's *angduhtrwacatsankceasesettweetnuffdease.*"

The class, biting nails, chewing tics, picking noses, listened respectfully to the strange sounds coming down Owd Corran's long, thin nose. Everybody was convinced, except me.

"Sir..."

He didn't want to know.

"<u>Sit</u> down and <u>keep</u> <u>quiet</u>."

That was my first, unenlightening contact with French pronunciation. It would never have struck Owd Corran that something might have been made of an eight-year-old boy who went to the trouble of writing for a free French lesson and trying to learn it.

I sat out the rest of the class in a daze, for some reason or other writing "les doigts" over and over again on an exercise book.

When the bell went, the class were all over me, and somebody started shouting,

"Hey, look at this! LES DOIGTS! He must be potty! LES DOIGTS! What does it mean?"

I got it all afternoon, at playtime and on the way home, but I finally shook them off.

In the back bedroom, on the little wooden bed under the window, lay a thin booklet. On the back it said, A MAN WHO KNOWS TWO LANGUAGES IS TWICE AS GOOD AS A MAN WHO ONLY KNOWS ONE.

I could still hear the jeers.

He's potty!

Owd Corran showed him all right!

Did you see what he'd written all over his book? "Les doigts!"

I crammed the little booklet into my jacket pocket and ran out into the back street, climbed the stone steps into Stansfield Street and set off for Boldventure Park, still climbing higher.

Up through the top park I climbed, on to the moors, up on to the high skyline where there was nothing but the Tower and the clean wind, and a crouching grouse-keeper in plus-fours watching me suspiciously through his glasses.

And there, looking out to where, thirty miles away, the Ribble glittered into the sea, I shouted French to the curlews.

"Les doigts! Les ongles!" I shouted,

"Un! dukes! troyz! quart! sink! six! sept! hewit! newf! dicks!..."

"Onz!" I shouted, "dooze! trys! quatters! quins! seas!

dicks-sept! dicks-hewit! dicks-newf! vingt!"

And still shouting, arms and legs pumping down the steep black shale path, I ran home to poison and chips.

Untitled 3

The sun lies thinly on the leaves,

no more than bread-and-scrape.

The air is used up on the fire escape.

Smuts cruise and settle on my rolled-up sleeves.

On the spare lot a gartered cat

nudges blackened clumps aside.

No normal creature tries to hide

as inefficiently as that;

small and jerseyed bundles chopping stones

must take their pleasure where they can;

the widow of the clothes-club man

will make and mend no bones.

Up above us in the sky

the giant chimney-stack explodes

and dirty boiler suits boil by

along the dogfouled roads.

The boot stamps out a hullabaloo

until the starter wakes or breaks.

Spreadeagled metal warms and shakes,

exhaust pipes gargle fumes of blue:

and I think of old walls, in a new way,

layer and line and length,

and old masons, makers of old walls,

their old, brown, wry-necked strength:

dry-wallers, working under the curlew's half-heard pipe,

half-seeing dried sheep's droppings, bog cotton, and plain snipe.

I think of old walls, blotched and spotted with yeast,

green, yellow and grey,

think of stone-stored sunshine, released

into the night air, like the smell of day.

Old walls, moonlit beneath leaf-scattered moonlight

or on the moors, most natural of made things:

sinewy, satisfied hands and minds compiled

their magic meanderings.

Scouting for Boys

I can't actually remember leaving the cubs and joining the scouts.

Some queer things happened at the time, but I don't think I'd go so far as to say they changed my life and had an important influence on my future development, such as it was. In fact, I think I *would go* so far as to say that they *didn't*, except for reading the *Champion Annual For 1925*, You never know though.

I liked the cubs. I liked our *Akela*, Florrie. She was short and crisp and had a nice smile, and she told us she had a slouch through carrying a heavy satchel of books when she was a schoolgirl. I don't remember the slouch. I don't think we knew what it meant. She was probably just showing off. But I still think she deserved a better fate than becoming a nun called *Sister Bonaventura* or some such name. It was through her I first heard the Jungle Book stories. She was a good reader, and I remember her doing Raksha the Demon baring her teeth at Shere Khan. I didn't mind the dib-a-dib bits, even the "Baloo the Bear" dance, though some of the kids thought it was a bit sickening, and I liked the treasure hunts for Woolie's toshies arranged by Miss Barber, who I thought of then rather the way I think of Julie Andrews - or perhaps Roberts - now.

We went to camp once up on the moors at *Owd Aggie's*, about half-a-mile from town, just for the night. My Dad turned up with a bar of that new white chocolate for me and to see that I was 'aw reet'. Nobody else's Dad turned up, just mine. I expect my mother had a hand in it somewhere. I got my eyes red and swollen with smoke, trying to fry stewing beef.

I remember some of us standing gaping at an old woman who had fallen next to the chip shop at the bottom of Radford and was trying to get up. Suddenly Florrie elbowed fiercely through us and pulled the old girl upright.

Then she laced into us.

She told us that there wasn't a gentleman among us. None of us had ever thought there was, but I began to wonder whether I was missing anything by not being one.

Anyway, it was all education. We now knew that gentlemen picked old women up. Another time she caught me peeing in a big arch right in the middle of Johnny Wraith Broo and told me angrily that I should be doing it in private up against a wall. Even dogs went in corners, she said.

I think that marked the final collapse of my innocence. I saw that I had to have a fig leaf on. Oh, and she took us to a big jamboree at Billinge End in Blackburn, where we saw Lord Bathing Towel (we believed the big lad who told us, I think he was called something Joyce) and about twenty thousand of us all shouted "Thief! Thief! Thief!" at him.

At least that is what it sounded like.

It made a big impression on me.

When I joined the scouts, I hadn't got all my uniform at first as it cost a packet of money. My cub uniform was a neckerchief and a woggle, both new, and a green cub-cap with faded yellow piping on it bought about third or fourth hand from my chum Tom Marsden's older brother *Bimbo*.

Bimbo had a lot bigger head than me, in fact he had a lot bigger head than anybody, so the back of the cap hung like a flap nearly to my neckerchief at the back. I looked as though I were in the Foreign Legion. As Bimbo had had ringworm in it and had to have his head shaved, my mother very sensibly put the cap on the dresser in the front bedroom for a week or two filled with Fuller's Earth. It looked like a soft plant pot. I still don't know what Fuller's Earth was (or is), but I didn't get ringworm on my head, though I once got one on my thigh and I used to go to the school clinic to get it painted with iodine. Like a little Catherine wheel, it was.

Then I got to join the scouts. At the first scout meeting I went to, some of *us* started climbing on the school wall next to the church pad, and I fell off and pulled a big copingstone off the top of the wall on to my left leg. While I doubt if it would ever have happened with Florrie in charge, I can't blame anybody but myself. Two scouts walked me home between them, Jud Wilkinson and Jackie Warden, I think. I hopped all the way with my arms round their necks.

My leg burned like fire all night. Doctor Costello looked over his stomach at it, and at Blackburn Infirmary it turned out to be "a fracture of the left tibia". They put a white plaster Wellington boot on it. We went to the Infirmary by tram - I actually raced my mother to the tram at the Boundary with a broken leg - but we came home in a taxi. I'd never been in a car before, let alone a taxi, so I remember it well. I don't know whether Mother had. How she ever managed to pay for a long run to the next town in those days, - and we went more than once - I don't know. But I think we were insured with the News Chronicle for a pound or two.

At home they made a bed for me downstairs out of two armchairs my Dad had made with his tool chest. I suppose he followed some kind of drawing from *The Amateur Mechanic*, which was the only book he actually owned apart from *Riders of the Purple Sage*. The end drawer of the dresser downstairs was full of Bible, all in loose bits that we darkly suspected Dad used to stuff out the front of his cap with, but it turned out to be the *Northern Daily Telegraph* he used, screwed up in a sort of banana shape. I don't know why. Anyway, the chairs looked pretty much as though Dad. had made them up out of his head. The back of each was a flat board which you leaned against at an angle of about a hundred degrees. There was a bit of wood nailed at the rear of each seat to stop the back sliding down. The seat was a flat board as well, but I think there was some sort of cushion on it, usually hiding old copies of the *Empire News*.

There were vertical wooden bars round the sides with flat arm-rests on top. When the two chairs were placed face-to-face, they made a kind of outsize cot where I lay looking at my plaster cast.

My mother had bought an enormous pair of zip-up carpet slippers, so that I could have one over the end of the cast. The other just disappeared. It would have fitted over Bimbo's head.

The best thing that came out of my accident was that old Mrs Howard next door gave my mother a book for me to read. It was *The Champion Annual For 1925*. All this happened in the late thirties, but I can still remember the pleasure I got out of that book, shining over everything I have read since, with Panther Grayle, Sexton Blake, Farraday Farr, story after priceless story. Scouts came to see me, too, Jud Wilkinson and Jackie Warden and Vic Gavaghan the assistant scoutmaster, bringing a wave of glamour and a copy of *Scouting for Boys* and a little Morse code buzzer with a battery and a coil and a contact. I lay there buzzing and reading Baden Powell's amazing tips on how to tell character by the way a boy wore down his heels, and his warning that a quiff of hair on your forehead was "a sure sign of silliness".

I read *Scouting for Boys* from cover to cover, looking forward with high hopes to taking an active and even distinguished part in the development of the Scout Movement. I began to comb my hair differently. My mother wasn't as interested in that as she was in getting some mysterious money from the newspapers. It appeared that I was insured with one newspaper for £10 and with another for £2, which can't have been much, even then. In order to collect the money, she had to have the scoutmaster's signature. I can't recollect his name now, especially as he was known to the scouts as *Skip* and to the louts as *Lickle Tashy*, an unlovely phrase coined by a big lad with a huge quiff who was himself commonly known as Dirty Bill.

Getting Lickle Tashy's signature was not easy. The only person who seemed to know where he lived, in Blackburn somewhere, was Jackie Warden, and Jackie darkly suspected that Mother had plans to "summons» the scoutmaster for neglect. When she asked him for the address, he claimed to have forgotten both the street and the number. On the other hand, he could explain how you got there.

The rigmarole seemed to go on for hours, something like this: "You know where the Empire is, where it like turns up to the Infirmary, well, you go that way, only you don't turn up to the Infirmary. Just before you get to the Empire there's like a road what goes up to the left round a pub and it goes out into the country and right round Tockholes, if you do go that way I mean, only there's like a tram stop outside this pub where you could get off if you went by tram. The road *you* want is the one that goes straight on past the Empire up to Redlam, only you don't go anywhere near Redlam, really..."

Mother just sat looking at him and his nerve broke. He made one desperate attempt to get off the hook by blurting out, "You see, missis, I allus go by bike, so I remember it as a bike ride. You'd be able to find it a lot easier if you went on a bike,"

My mother couldn't keep her face straight any longer." Ee, Jackie, love," she said, "Can you *see* me pedalling to Blackburn on a bike?" She laughed herself red in the face, and I laughed with her.

The idea of my mother on a bike was as good as Wheeler and Wolsey, and "Can you see me on a bike, Jackie love?" became a family classic, one for the air raid shelter.

I suppose the joke is just as hard to grasp today as it is to understand how you could be insured with a newspaper for £2. Still, as I wrote this, my mother was still laughing at Jackie's suggestion. The first time I saw my mother-in-law cycling about, half as heavy again and much older than Mother was at that time, I thought what a headache she would have been for Jackie.

When they took the cast off my leg eight weeks later, all the hairs on the leg came off with it agonizingly and my foot floated slowly up towards the ceiling. Shod in a new pair of high boots, I took the tram home with my mother. I sat upstairs at the front all the way up the Cravens and didn't miss the taxi at all. I don't suppose Mother did either. It was typical of her that she spent some of the precious £12 we got from the newspapers on new scout clothes for me with *Bukta* stamped all over them. I already had a neckerchief and a woggle. In place of Bimbo's gigantic cub cap, I got a real Scout hat with a broad brim and a leather hand round it. When I read some years ago that the Scouts had decided to wear berets because the old hats made them feel silly, it brought back with a rush the feeling I had the first time I caught sight of my silhouette with the glamorous scout hat on in Slinger's butcher's window at the top of Cochran Street. Gladys Morrell wore a beret. I was a scout! And the money stretched to a new scout belt with a three-leafed clover on the buckle, a white lanyard encircling my neck and plaited into my neckerchief ending in a bronze whistle clipped on belt and balanced on the other side by a sheath-knife with a ball on top. I even had a khaki shirt with pockets and green garter- tabs.

I also had a non-regulation wart between my eyes at the root of my nose which my mother used to colour purple with a wet match head to burn it away. It added to the drama of my appearance, perhaps.

At any rate it didn't prevent me trailing; clouds of glory all the way to the school. The scoutmaster, I discovered, wanted, to get out of the school and into a proper scout den, a more colourful place with our own flags on display, bits of bark and woodwork, something more exciting than rows of desks.

I honestly didn't care.

Swaggering about in uniform was as far as I had got. Flags and woodwork were for the future. I remember one glamorous remark which seemed to promise great things to come however. It was about Jud Wilkinson.

Somebody said. admiringly, "Jud's mother always knows when he's off camping - she just goes to look if the oven-plate is missing. Jud always uses it to stiffen his saddlebag with when he packs for camp."

I felt the hair rising on the back of my neck as I pictured myself stiffening my very own saddlebag with our oven-plate. To tell the truth, up to then I had associated our oven-plate with being warm in bed, because my Dad used to wrap it up in newspaper and put it on our big flock mattress to warm our feet.

It reminded me of cries of "Hey, 'udge up a bit Our Margaret, and let's have a bit o't th'oven-plate!" Later we moved on to the more sophisticated stage of using "stone" sarsaparilla bottles to warm up the bed. Everybody except Dad, that is.

Somewhere off Bolton Road was a ghastly place called Maitland Street. I very much hope it disappeared long ago. At the time however I thought of it differently because that was where our scout den was. I carried buckets of water from the old slopstone at the back all one Saturday afternoon and helped to scrub the bare flagstones in the front room which was very pokey and cold.

We had a couple of candles burning, and to tell the truth, the thing I now remember best was that Jackie Warden could hold his hand six inches over a candle and get his palm blackened with the smoke without getting burned. I wasn't surprised when I read some years later that he had been a awarded a medal for bravery in the fire brigade. The old slum had. never had such a face-lift before, but I was glad to get home, especially as my Dad was taking me to see a "Yankee film". I think he must have been one of the last people to use the expression.

On Monday morning we had a visit from the *Father* and the tip-up seats crashed back almost as one as we sprang rigidly to attention.

Father Muldoon inspired our most dramatic performance because we were all scared speechless of him. He was long and lank and brown, or rather yellow, and to my half-baked mind anyway, he looked like Boris Karloff's big brother. He was electrifying in the pulpit. I can see him now, throwing up his long bony arms, filling the church with a great cry coming out of his lantern jaws over the packed rows of faces:

"God made the sun, the moooon and the staaars!"

One of the biggest shocks I ever had was opening the front door and finding on the doorstep, not Milner Hatpin with a pile of grubby comics to swop, but Father Muldoon. I took one terrified look up at his stern features, saw in a flash that there was no more possibilty of communication with him than there is between man and vampire bat, and dashed in shouting *"It's the Father!"*

I then ran straight out of the back gate, up the back street steps, and stood staring down from the overhead railings at the bottom of Stansfield Street into the yard, with bulging eyes. Mother went out to the front door to meet him, wiping soapsuds off her elbows. The story went that Dad once told a priest who walked in without knocking to get out and knock. When the priest remarked "But I am your spiritual father", Dad told him "I've only got one feyther, and he lives in Hacking Street. " So, he only laughed when he heard about my escape, but my mother really gave it me.

The first thing the Father did when we had settled into our seats again was to read my name out. I felt only slightly less ill when he read out several more names and it turned out he wanted to see all the boy scouts alone in turn in Owd Danny's classroom next door.

"Come in, come in, may chayld," he called out in a great yellow voice as I sidled round the door wearing a jersey with a matching tie which I used to chew in moments of stress. (My mother once tried to cure me by giving me a plate of bits of tie for my dinner). He smiled at me benevolently (I've never understood this craze for horror films. They fail to grip you when you've known the real thing).

"Sit down, may chayld, sit down;" he came and stood over me. He was about nine foot six. Can he really have been wearing black gloves?

"Now, may chayld, you know that I have only your spiritual good at heart, he told me, "So when I ask you to give me your solemn, holy and binding word never to go to any more of these scout meetings, I know you will do so at once without any hesitation.".

He didn't say why. I didn't need to know why. I would have promised to steal my mother's purse just to get out of there. I am astounded at a dim recollection that I actually asked the Father why. Perhaps I didn't really do it and have got it all mixed up with reading a lot of Dickens of the " He wos werry good. to me, he wos " kind. But that is how I remember it, and when I got the answer that, ah – "there was reason to believe that the scoutmaster was not a very good. influence..." my memory even tells me that I cried a bit and told him that the scouts had been to see me when I had a broken leg and nobody else came near. Perhaps only the tears were real, but any rate, when I left the room my scouting career, such as it was, was over.

Dirty Bill explained to me later in considerable detail just how "Lickle Tashy" had been scouting for boys, but I couldn't tell my mother that, and she just put it down to the fact that the priests didn't want the scout group to get away from their influence. It doesn't worry me anymore.

I don't remember ever seeing the scoutmaster after that, though I once saw Jud Wilkinson pedalling up Bull Hill into the wind with an enormous saddlebag behind him, well stiffened with his mother's oven plate.

I still have the whistle and the woggle, though the hat has been missing for ages, and my chances of going camping are pretty slim these days, unless I can get a longer flex on my electric blanket.

....

PS . I read somewhere later that Eisenhower's bedroom , a US showpiece , displayed his bedside book . It was Zane Grey's *Riders of the Purple Sage*.

Gravy Eyes

When I were a lad, it was a disgrace to get into debt. Everything was sort of upside-down then, compared with today. If you have a big debt today, it's something to be proud of, the inflation is working for you and that. If you just save money, you are "half-way up Brandy-House Broo", as people used to say. I think that was where the workhouse was. If you want to understand how I felt about our debts, you have to try to feel what a disgrace it was but not quite manage it. I mean, I didn't know why it was a disgrace, I just know it was because my mother felt that way and it rubbed off on the rest of us.

As a matter of fact, we hardly had any debts. to start with, there was no mortgage because very few ordinary working people owned their own houses. I know we didn't. We belonged to the off-licence next door and paid a weekly rent. I doubt whether we ever owed much rent, because it would have been a bit awkward getting behind and living next door to your landlord, especially when you did your buying-in there. Sometimes Mother got a bit fed up with feeling obliged to buy in there when it was cheaper "down't street" - that is, in the town centre. She did save something by shopping in town, but it was a long pull up Johnny Wraith Broo with a couple of carrier-bags. Carrier-bags were stout brown paper bags with string handles that cut your fingers. Besides, the shop next door was handy for Black-and-Green's tea or gas-mantles, for lung-healers and packets of Star. My Dad smoked ten Star a day and I got the cigarette cards to play knock-down and slitch-on with.

People in streets like ours had two rooms and a scullery downstairs and lived in the back room. The front room was for visitors and great occasions only, with a three-piece suite, brass fireirons, and swarms of framed photographs. Our front room was different. It was really nice. It had just lino, a couple of broken chairs, some rope and a lot of interesting junk.

It was a nice place to play in when you didn't need a fire. It was a bit on the musty side, perhaps, but you could put your soldiers up without anybody standing on them and my younger sister Parge had her dollies in there. I passed many a happy Sunday there sticking soldiers' heads back on with matchsticks.

Nobody knew how much my mother hated it and wanted a proper front room, but one day I came home from school and found it had been turned into a fairyland. There was a new carpet, a big three-piece leather suite with rolled arms and great stuffed velvet seats. There was a polished gate-legged table and a set of heavy mahogany chairs. There was a new sideboard with fancy metal handles and a secret drawer in one of the cupboards we only discovered later. On the sideboard stood a polished rose-bowl with a silver crisscross netting on top, and two tall, polished metal flower-vases, the kind you never put flowers in.

Fifty pounds it had cost, altogether. I heard later that my mother had just gone out and ordered it all without Dad even knowing, and that there was a lot of shouting, but I saw Dad going into the front room afterwards, running his big fingers carefully along the edge of the sideboard and sitting down in the corner of the sofa. Then he looked up and said, "We'll have to have a fire in here on Sunday. It's a bit damp." You could see he was suited.

I might be quite wrong thinking it was this fifty pounds we had to pay back to the loan office because most shops handled their own hire-purchase in those days, but at any rate I used to be given an envelope with a weekly instalment in it to take to "the Loan". Mother used to brief me carefully for the trip. I mustn't on any account let anybody see me go in. I had to wait until there was nobody about and then go in quick. When I came out, I had to look both ways and then run for it. I felt that the good name of the family was on my shoulders.

"The Loan" was a small office a hundred yards off the main road, down a side street. I daren't go that way, but if I went up Railway Road and round the back of the library and down the side of the technical school - a bristling forest of green railings - I could get to the office from the other end of the street. It was a long way round for short legs. I crept along hiding in door-holes on the last stretch and then burst into the office so fast that I fell on the floor. A pinched face looked at me over a partition through little oval spectacles and asked me what I wanted.

I got up with a red face. It was like talking to the Devil. There he was, sitting in the middle of his shameful den, a place you crept into and out of in the shadows with your face hidden. I handed him a crumpled brown envelope. He looked at it doubtfully. He had the kind of moustache which looked as though it had come down his nose. He took some money out of the envelope and a little book. He wrote something in the book, stamped it from a purple ink pad and gave it to me again without a word. I pointed to the envelope, and he thrust it at me. I stuffed everything into my jacket pocket, turned up my coat collar and went out. A fat lady with a carrier bag came past. It said *Home and Colonial* on the carrier bag. I turned round to face the wall while she passed me, and when I looked again, she was watching me over her shoulder.

A more normal feature of our daily life was the clothes club man. A clothes club was a firm which advanced you money in the shape of a large, theatrical-looking cheque which could be used to buy clothing with. You paid it back so much a week. Mother didn't seem to be particularly ashamed about the clothes club man (or men, seeing that there were several of them) coming round. Perhaps it was because ours wasn't by any means the only house they came to, and perhaps because you couldn't do anything about it anyway. I mean, you couldn't ask the clothes club man to go round the back. One of them was Mr. Hutchinson, who was tall and lean in a bowler hat and dark overcoat. He looked like John Buchan and was gentlemanly.

Another, Mr Tiller, was short, redfaced, bignosed and goggling, with a funny furry trilby and a shabby raincoat. Every time he came, he laid his hat carefully on the table while he noted down the weekly payment, and then told us about it before he put it back on his head. It was a genuine Borsalino or something and he had had it for an amazing length of time, perhaps twenty years. Every few years he wore it the other way round to save wear and tear on the brim. His raincoat was also a genuine something, a Burberry, possibly. I used to think he told us about his expensive clothes just to rub it in that he didn't have to join a clothing club.

One hot summer day his raincoat sleeve went into a big jug of homemade lemonade standing on the table to cool, and when he had gone, Mother poured the whole jugful down the sink. She was always inventing names for people, and she used to call Mr.Tiller Toby Tortoise, so we did as well, and that sort of thing can cause trouble. There was also a very small, sad-looking clothes club man with watery pouches under his eyes. I forget his real name, but mother called him Gravy Eyes. She knew she was being wicked, but she had to make her own fun, and besides, she was part Welsh. Of course, it had to happen. I went to the door one day, all of seven years old, found the sad little man standing on the top step and shouted "Mother! it's Gravy Eyes!"

Clothes club cheques were only accepted by certain shops, and you were given a list, which was sometimes out of date. We always seemed to go to the same two boring places, boring to me, anyway. There was Nancy Jepson's up Redearth Road, and Mr. Gray's "down't street" - that is, in the middle of town. I probably wasn't much of an expert on what were good clothes shops and what weren't. Nancy Fenton's, as I recall it, was a little place down some steps all hung with flowered pinnies. We went there for things like girls' dresses, ordinary ones in cotton and posher ones in some stuff called organdie, I think. Nancy Fenton looked a bit like Gracie Fields. What used to surprise me, and still does, was how any woman could tell whether one of those shapeless bags on coat-hangers was worth trying on or not. Perhaps they couldn't, and that was why there *was* such a lot of trying on. I used to wander about looking at dresses with arrows and flaps on and striped flannel pyjamas. At Mr. Gray's we got clothes for my Dad and sometimes me. I used to get hairy blazers and navy-coloured trousers which were held up by braces or a snake-buckle belt from Woolworth's, came down over my knobbly little knees and hurt me in between my legs. They were called "boy's knickers". I didn't like the idea of wearing knickers. I didn't even wear underpants as a matter of fact; perhaps that is why the boy's knickers hurt me in between my legs.

Mr. Gray was a plump, over-polite man who talked like the actors in one of those British films nobody went to, with *Hulbert*s in them. He used to wear gold-rimmed spectacles, a blue serge suit, and a silver tie. The worst part of it all for me was the polite conversation while he wrapped up what we had bought in brown paper parcels, and the agonizing bit where my mother produced the badge of our shame, the clothing club cheque. My dad wasn't a bit of help because he had some sort of crushing complex which made him quite unable to face people like Mr. Gray and his silver tie. God knows how he was brought up. He had to go to that shop because they took the cheques, but it took a lot out of mother getting him inside. He would try on what they had, which was always hopelessly ill-fitting. For one thing, there wasn't the variety of ready-made clothes then that there is now, especially if you only had one shop to choose from, and Dad wouldn't have gone anywhere else. For another, Dad was a pocket Hercules, a type commoner in those days.

He was an extreme case, too, with a lot of weightlifting and Lancashire-style wrestling behind him. His great ideal was George Hackenschmidt, and one of the great regrets of his life was that he was put on the same bill as Hackenschmidt in London in a supporting bout and couldn't get the fare together. Only a good made-to-measure suit would have fitted him, but he never got one.

Mr. Gray used to go through the same rigmarole every time, measuring Dad's big chest and narrow waist and shaking his head and saying his bit about Dad's measurements being those of one man in a thousand. When you come to think of it though., Mr. Gray's portly belly was more likely to have been that of one man in a thousand in a hard-up working-class district like ours. Dad stood there poker-faced, but if you knew him you could see he liked it. All "body-builders" like that sort of thing. I had had enough of Dad and his weights. ("just watch that muscle. See it go up and down?" "Yes, dad. Can I have a tuppenny comic, dad?")

He always ended up with a blue serge suit, the jacket stretched across his shoulders and upper arms like rubber and the trousers wide enough for a pillow down the front. Then he'd say, "Well, I have to go and see about that theer..." and make his escape, leaving my mother fumbling in her bag for the shameful clothes club cheque.

I must have been out of boy's knickers for a while when Mother took me to Blackburn for new clothes one cold winter's day that threatened snow. We walked all the way up Whalley Range, and finally found a shop. She really let herself go, buying things for me, as she would never have done for herself. She must have bought things for herself too, but all I can remember was a hat that Dad said made her look like "a bloody U-boat commander". (It was known ever after as "the U-boat" even by mother herself.)

I got a rust-coloured sports coat with imitation leather buttons, brown shoes, a shirt, and a pair of "slacks" in a kind of cloudy grey stuff. When Mother bought me a "military raincoat" as well, covered with straps and buttons, I felt that the world would shortly be seeing the real me. I was about to move up in the pecking order. I was so delighted that for once I had quite forgotten the moment of truth I always dreaded, and was completely aghast at hearing the query, "You take clothes club cheques, don't you?" parried with the reply, "Oh no, we haven't taken them for a long time now". After everything had been parcelled up, too. We shuffled out into the wind. We went down King William Street, Mother swearing at the clothes club all the way for not keeping us up to date with its list. We sometimes had our tea out when we went to Blackburn, but that day we hadn't enough. I thought about the rust-coloured sports coat so nearly mine. I still wonder at times who got it instead of me. Suddenly, on the outside market ground, Mother put her foot on something quick, and stood looking round her for a good while before she bent down and picked up a ten-shilling note. Her eyes were the brightest in Blackburn that afternoon, which perhaps isn't saying much. "Come on, love," she said, "we're having our tea out today at Greenwood's!" And we did. It didn't quite make up for the loss of a military raincoat, but it helped.

Owd Corran, Owd Danny

At St. Joseph's in Darwen there was Owd Corran. He wasn't called Owd Corran except by all the kids. He was called Mr. Yates. (Somebody once told me there was something called Yates's Corrans (currants). His wife for some inscrutable reason was called Madam Yates. I think she sang and was fat (the two things sort of went together) and she wore one of those fox-fur collars featuring a little fox's head with beady glass eyes. No, I don't know what for, and it doesn't matter anyway, except that it looked a bit as though she had two heads.

They also had this sissy kid called Geoffrey with sort of pale gold hair with a side parting, and a pink scar on his nose where he had been punched or fell. Probably punched. (Yes, I am well aware that practically nobody was called 'Geoffrey ' then, though years later I heard a plump Mum on the sands at Blackpool near the Teapot shouting to her son "Joff, come on over here, Joff." She had had him christened Geoffrey because it was posh, without even knowing how you said it.)

Well, so there was Owd Corran droning on and on about the *Ob* the *Lena* and the *Yenesei,* tapping an old cracked oil cloth map of Eurasia thrown over the permanently chalky blackboard while the mice ran crackling backwards and forwards between a big hole they'd chewed in the waste-paper basket and their nest behind the hot-water pipes with drinking straws. (We drank our milk through real straws in those days not twisted paper or plastic.)

Owd Corran had one nasty habit; he used to blow his nose in an extremely filthy old snotrag, then he'd stuff it into his pants pocket while we watched in fascinated disgust. It might not sound like much, but believe it, it was quite unforgettable.

He wasn't much of a teacher, to be honest, but he must have been observant enough to see I wasn't getting much out of his slow tutelage, or to be honest, maybe he was just fed up with me. So, it was suggested I take a quick skip and jump up to Mr. Pennington's class instead.

Although I rather liked the idea of being put up into a class with boys older than me, I was dismayed at the very idea of being in Mr. Pennington's class. For one thing, Owd Danny had these yellow teeth like somebody in Dickens and you could smell his breath from across the classroom. The funny thing was than once I got into his class, it never bothered me at all, and he turned out to be a grand teacher.

Owd Danny applied what has come to be called the *Tom Sawyer Whitewash* trick. If you tell a kid to clean the blackboard or empty the wastepaper basket, he might think you were picking on him. But if you make it a competition so the kid who is smartest and sits up straightest with his arms folded get the job of reading the thermometer or cleaning the blackboard, then they fight for it: "Sir! Sir! Sir!"

"*Control* is the motto for today", he used to tell us every morning. Later on, all he had to do was to ask when he walked in what the motto for today was.

"Sir! Control is the motto for today, sir!" we shouted. Nobody had the faintest idea what it meant.

Owd Danny introduced or at any rate extended the clean hands league idea. You came to school looking clean and tidy with your face washed, your hair combed stiffly back in a becoming, vaselined quiff, and your hands held out for inspection. Tommy Dolan always won; he was Danny's favourite. He was naturally pink and clean, smallish and chubby-faced but not a bit sissy because there weren't any at our school, apart from me, I mean. (Owd Corran's kid "Geoffrey" didn't go to our school).

Tommy was in fact a keen cricketer and one of those twinkling-footed football fans who knew all the names, Len Hutton, Denis Compton and so on. His hero wasn't Owd Danny, but Stanley Matthews, as it ought to have been. His older cousin Johnny was a bit *doolally*. The prize for having the cleanest hands was a bit of satin ribbon to sew on your lapels. There were different colours – perhaps they stood for different things like the D.S.C. and the V.C. but as I never won any, I don't remember. (I think the "V.C." was actually a little badge from the clean hands league with a pair of clean hands on it or something). Anyway, Tommy's lapels with all the rows of ribbons sewn on presumably by a proud Mum (though you never knew with Tommy) outshone Kaiser Bokassa and Goering put together.

I once came top in the exams though (it didn't mean much), and in Owd Danny's class (but nowhere else) there were prizes. The first prize was an old tin whistle and the second prize a nice shiny brown wooden "bird call" whistle. I won the tin whistle, much to my disgust.

My mother was pleased with my report but wouldn't let me have the whistle on the typical motherly grounds that you never knew who else had been blowing it. And when I remembered Owd Danny's yellow teeth and awful breath, I was inclined to agree.

He once asked me for some reason if I was interested in poetry, and (of course) I told him I was. "I have a poetry book for you, I'll bring it tomorrow" he promised. It was only a poetry book, but I was quite excited about it, though I got to sleep all right.

However, it turned out to be a much-faded green-backed jumble-sale copy of *The Poems of William Cowper*. My mother, who loved poetry, the real stuff like like *The Graves of a Household* or *She's Coming. She's Coming, Sweet Maggie* or *Edinburgh After Flodden* was also disappointed.

"Who the heck is William Cow-per?" (She pronounced it the sensible way)

" Who's ever heard of William Cow-per?"

It seemed to be all one long poem called "*The Task*". I never found out what the task was, unless it was *trying to find out* what the task was.

Anyway, Owd Danny's book was lying about somewhere or other for years, at least part of the time in the coal shed, along with a copy of *Westward Ho!* I bought at a school jumble sale for tuppence. I got sucked in there, though, because the middle forty pages were missing. I expect I could put my hand on both books if you want them and you have a towel waiting. Actually, Danny's class not only learned some poems by heart, but acted them out as well.

I remember Joe Harrison, a big bulldog-faced lout who one wouldn't have thought was any good at anything except twisting your arm up your back, giving electrifying recitals of poems, with actions. I remember him doing *Sir Ralph the Rover* in Southey's *The Inchcape Rock,* stalking across the classroom, holding a rolled up paper to his eye as a telescope and roaring out the lines:

"Sir Ralph the Rover walked the deck:

And fixed his eye, on the farther speck!"

Joe's masterpiece though was "The King Cophetua" in Tennyson's *The Beggar Maid.* As I had only just moved up into Danny's class, I couldn't quite catch Joe's rhetoric, but to me it sounded like:

"Ko-fett-you-ah sware a royal oath: THIS VEGGER-VAY SHALL VEE MY KVEE!"

What it meant was a mystery to me, but it was quite unforgettable.

Joe was good at acting poems, and proud of it, though I don't suppose he had much use for his talent in his later career, which unfortunately included following Fon McGlynn round the moors and shouting abuse at him. Joe wasn't really bright enough to realise (a) that Fon knew who he was *and* (b) that after the holidays, *he* would be in Fon's class. Fon had him sitting all day writing out a poem or something called "Courtesy". I suppose it took Joe all day (at least) to write it out once.

Danny knew how to handle Joe Harrison, but not Joe Middlehurst, who sat one day crying all over his exercise book, making great ink blots. and shouting something or other. Somebody told me Joe was crying because Owd Danny had insulted his mother or something, which was about as unlikely as it gets. (I think she'd just died).

But there were brighter moments, especially under the tutorship of Mathematics teacher Alfonso 'Fon' McGlynn, as good a teacher as I've ever had.

I remember vividly his choirboys outing; a rousing game of cricket followed by a walk, ending up at the cinema in the balcony with a bar of Needler's gritty chocolate each - I can still taste it. Greta Nissen was in a highly unsuitable movie called *Jamboree*. All I can recall of it now was a number of womens arms moving erotically up and down a sort of silver-fringe curtain to moans of "Jam-bor-ee! Jam-bor-ee!"

Mr McGlynn didn't like it much. If he could have, he'd have put a postcard in front of the lens as he used to during the spicier bits of the old movies he showed us in the science room after benediction on Wednesday nights. We saw T*he Cabinet of Dr. Caligari* and Fritz Lang's *Metropolis* and a Charlie Chaplin (the Policeman Charlie one) backwards.

He could 'rag out' *You're the Top* on the piano as he felt like, but choir-wise he used to go in for the posher hymns like "Veni Sancte Spi-i-ri-tus/ Et emitte cæ-æ-æ-litus/ Lucis tuae ra-a-a-dium"

God only knew what it all meant, but then we were singing it for God anyway, so that was all right.

Fon McGlynn went into the Raff as a navigator and was shot down over Berlin, so I heard. His sister played hell with the priest Father Hughes, who brought in his unprepossessing brother as headmaster when Owd Tipping left. Miss McGlynn thought her brother should have got the job and a deferment:

"You don't care whose brother ends up as cannon fodder as long as yours is safe!" she is reputed to have yelled at him.

Fon

Fon McGlynn. Who? Fon McGlynn

died in a bomber over Berlin,

wore a Norfolk jacket and walked on his toes

all sallow skin and Spanish jaw,

wrote an ironic Irish prose

and loved the rule of law.

When Fon McGlynn explained to me

the joke about hagiology,

the science-room slates curled and uncurled.

I had a fulcrum now to press the world.

Why My Dad would only sit on the End Seat on the Back Row at the Pictures

I don't know why my Dad would only sit on the end seat on the back row at the pictures. Nor do I know why he always left before the picture was over, but it did something to me which I have never really got over.

We used to get there in good time so that we could sit on the back row. Not the back row of the balcony of course. That would have been far beyond our means, and besides. Dad could never have put up with the kissing and cuddling up there. No, I mean the back row of the stalls, just next to where the usherette used to stand with her torch under the little entrance light. I couldn't really *drown* in the film as long as those lights were there. One usherette used to stand with her lit torch level with her shoulder with the light shining down on her lovely blonde hair and making her nose look twice as big as usual, which wasn't at all necessary. She stood like that all the way through *King Kong*.

That was at the *Olympia*, which - so I once heard - could seat three thousand souls. It was the biggest cinema in a small cotton town which had no less than five when I were a lad, one of which, admittedly, was just a "laugh-and-scratch".

There was no television then, and people went to the pictures several times a week. On the wall of the Savoy, a longish tram-ride down Blackburn Road, was a very special poster under glass, showing a young lad, all lit up, crouching in a sort of convulsion, staring at a cinema screen and clutching the arms of his seat. Underneath it said something like:"No finer tribute can be paid to the MOTION PICTURE INDUSTRY than this: it has awakened the dreams and ambitions of youth". As there was a sort of spotlight playing on the lad while the rest of the audience was in shadow, it was easy for me to identify myself with him because of where we always sat.

The cinemas were always very respectable places in those far-off days when everybody took off their hats and kept their heads still. Rolling pop bottles under the seats in those days, to say nothing of throwing darts from the balcony, were dreams and ambitions of youth that hadn't yet been awakened. Besides, you would have got clumped round the ear, because the whole cinema was full of muscle in those days before fork-lift trucks and digging machines. It was rather like being in church, but more fun, usually.

My Dad and my mother never went to the pictures together, partly because they couldn't afford to take us all if they did, and a couple didn't go off to the pictures in those days and leave the children at home. It would have been like going to Blackpool without them. But it was also because Mother wouldn't sit on the next-to-the-end seat on the back row. I liked going with her and getting right into the middle of a crowded cinema, right down in the dark, though you had to pass choc-ices and money backwards and forwards along your row during the interval. Luckily there wasn't a single fire scare in all my years at the pictures, from *Trader Horn* and *Manhattan Melodrama* and Tom Mix in *Destry Rides Again* (when I disgraced myself and my family by peeing under the seat with excitement) to Patricia Roc and Gordon Jackson in *Millions Like Us.* A fire would have been a catastrophe. Usually Mother went to pictures where you could have a "good cry", and whilst I quite liked these, I enjoyed cowboy films more, and they were the ones Dad went to, apart from those with Jimmy Cagney and Edward G. . His favourite Western actor - apart from Randolph Scott of course - was George O'Brien, who always wore black and looked as though he was holding a deep breath. "He's a fine figure of a man," Dad told me.

Sometimes there was what was called a continuous programme where the whole thing went round, and round from about six o'clock onwards. Perhaps it still does, though I don't go round with it any more. It was all right if there was, say, a musical film on, a Deanna Durbin or some such thing where the story didn't matter much. If there was a surprise ending though (the local Advertiser usually told you when there was}, you had to be careful to ask at the box office window whether the film was finishing or not, otherwise you got to know who *dun* it before you got to know what he *dun*.

I got badly sucked in like that in Llandudno once, perhaps because my Welsh wasn't so hot. They sent me inside after telling me it had only a couple of minutes to run, and I sat with my fingers in my ears looking at the floor and humming for ages before I discovered I had missed all the beginning of the film. The programme was continuous. The first time I was allowed to go to the pictures by myself, Dad saw me in, and would collect me afterwards. I forget the name of the film, but I remember Victor Maclaglen running about with a full-sized machine-gun on a tripod mowing down rows of soldiers, to put a boy king - it can only have been Freddie Bartholomew -back on his throne. *Ratatatatatatat*. I sat there glued to my own throne while the programme went round and round, until at last, late at night -. it must have been going on for eleven - a torch came wavering along the rows and playing on the wall, and a voice in the wilderness cried "Is there a little boy in here called Arthur Clayborough?" Once outside, the boy king got clumped all the way up Johnny Wraith Broo.

If you went to the pictures with Mother, there was always a chance that she might call in at the *Savoy Cafe* or the *Palladium Cafe*, depending on where *you* went, for a plate of chips and a bottle of Vimto on the way home. Dad was much too inhibited to go into places like that. The only time I can remember going anywhere with him after a film was when I was in air force uniform, when to my surprise he suggested washing the trail dust out of our throats - it must have been a Randolph Scott. film we had seen - at the *George*.

It was a belated recognition that I was growing up. After the preliminary evening-Harrys and is-that-your-lads, I committed the grave blunder of asking for a packet of crisps. Bluff working-men's faces turned pale all down the bar, and the landlord shook his head before disappearing for a considerable time. A great rusty tin box rose into view, the top was levered off with difficulty, and it was found to contain one limp, motheaten packet of "Tattis" which was fished out for me while Dad looked the other way. It was our first and last visit to a pub together.

Still, Dad usually saw to it that I had something to munch, or rather crunch, when we went to the pictures. The ice cream interval was still rather sketchy when I was a boy. One or two cinemas sent a girl round with tubs and choc-ices during the forthcoming attractions "trailers", but the usual thing was to take your own caramels or wine gums with you.

A regular local institution in those days was a poor chap with only one leg and a crutch who stood at the door of the cinema - usually at the rear entrance - with a big cumbersome home-made wooden tray round his neck and sold something called "cough candy" in square paper bags.

A wistful "Evenin' Harry" made it morally impossible for Dad to walk past without buying some "cough candy" and we always did.

It was called cough candy because it made you cough. Like the tray, it was rough, cumbersome home-made stuff, sometimes peaty-brown and sometimes shiny black. It seemed to be made of equal parts of sugar and coke and scratched *your* throat. It took quite an effort to get it down, and of course I had to eat the lot myself, though Dad used to pretend that he liked it.

It never dawned on me that I didn't *need* to eat it. It was toffee, the only toffee you were going to get, and you ate it even if it was awful. After all, sometimes the picture was awful, but nobody ever walked out in those days. You couldn't afford to throw money away like that. All the same, I didn't really look forward to those bags of cough candy, and it seemed to me that the one-legged salesman had an uncanny knack of guessing which cinema we were going to. It was a long way from the *Olympia* to the *Savoy* in those days before cars, but we met him at both places, to say nothing of the *Palladium*, the *Albert Hall* and the *Public Hall*.

The last one was the scruffiest of them all, and we only went there to see Hoot Gibson films. We sometimes sat next to a man with St.Vitus Dance who kept rubbing his shoulder with his chin. He probably sat on the back row because he couldn't keep his head still. I would find myself sitting between him and Dad, and I used to worry about catching whatever he had got. Of course, my Dad told me when I asked him that I couldn't catch anything, but what did *he* know?

I was very habit-prone anyway, and usually developed several new habits every year. I spent a whole summer for example patting my mouth with the tips of my fingers while I whistled through them. Another time I walked, about on my toes for a week or two, but I think that was through reading in a comic about somebody who "walked on the balls of his feet like a giant cat", though I didn't know what the balls of your feet were, and I'm not so sure about it now.

I did try rubbing my shoulder experimentally with my chin a few times, but it was one habit I didn't catch. I remember Dad nudging me one evening to give the St. Vitus' Dance man some cough candy, but he choked on it and had to be slapped on the back.

He had a cheery little lad with him who always sat on his other side, so I never got to know him.

Perhaps my Dad had some sort of oddity as well, seeing that he would only sit on the end seat on the back row. Perhaps it was claustrophobia, but at one time he had been a coal miner. Perhaps he didn't like standing up at the end for *God Save The King*, though he wasn't against royalty, and in fact I think he was rather in favour of them, though he never mentioned them except in rather weak jokes of the "God Save Queen George" type.

Mother once told me Dad had done so much fighting when he was younger that he wanted to be able to get out in a hurry if he was recognised, like a gunfighter sitting with his back to the wall, but I can't see that being the reason. For one thing, he was more recognizable right next to the lamp at the entrance than in the dark, and for another we hadn't got our backs to the wall but next to a passageway. And finally, he knew nearly everybody in town. And I expect they knew him. At any rate, when we walked up Railway Road in summer on our way to Blackpool carrying our big cardboard suitcase, it was like an imperial progress with all the "'Ow-do-Harrys" and "Off-then-are-you-Harrys".

It was far more likely he wanted to be off because he was an old Puritan and couldn't watch the final embrace. "Come on, tha' silly little begger" he'd say, pulling me to my feet and out of the exit while the angel choir swelled yearningly, the hero rowed the last few yards across the moonlit lake into his sweetheart's arms, and the attendants pulled back the big green drapes from the exits with a rattle of curtain rings. By the time The King came on, we were half-way up Johnny Wraith Broo.

I never got to see the words THE END.

Many years later when he was a pensioner, I took him to see a Western called *Ten Thousand On The Hoof* at the Albert Hall. By that time the old tip-up seats were worn with a great mange, though the cinema had a new name and management nearly every month: it was currently called *The Tudor*.

Dad leaned back contentedly and filled his pipe with St.Bruno Flake."I like a Western," he said, "They're a good clean film, are a Western." He sucked a bit before lighting up. "Do you know, I helped to build this place," he told me.

Unfortunately, as luck would have it, I had taken him to the wrong picture, an easy mistake to make in those days when the programme changed at least twice a week. What we had paid to see was a drama of searing passion called *Bad For Each Other* with Lizbeth Scott.

Dad drew a long breath and gave me the kind of stare from up under his eyebrows that used to frighten me when I was a small boy.

"I think we're bloody bad for each other," he told me disgustedly.

Every time the hero and heroine went into a clinch, which seemed to be excessively often even to me, Dad dropped his matches and groped for them under the seat, muttering fiercely. We finally broke the golden rule and came out before it was over. After all, it was my money. I can only remember taking Dad to the pictures, as against his taking me, one other tine, long after he had retired. We sat on the *front* row this time, but it was up in the balcony in splendid isolation at an afternoon "matinee". The film was a poor remake of *Farewell To Arms*. In the novel, the girl's death is described very briefly, but Jennifer Jones was married to the producer, and was determined to be "an unconscionable time a-dying". Just in front of us was a broad polished shelf which reflected the whole film upside down and seemed to make the death-scene even longer. Dad sat it out stolidly puffing at his pipe, but at last he had more than enough and burst out angrily,

"Ay, to hell with it, I wish oo'd get a move on and *snuff it.*"

Perhaps, after all, the reason why *my* Dad sat on the end seat on the back row at the pictures was that he couldn't face that awful shuffling-out to music when the lights go up at the end and you are booted straight out of heaven into a world of dirty raincoats and soiled hats. It is where you belong and where you deserve to be, but when you have just been riding the purple sage, it takes time to adjust to it again. In some of those old fire-traps it could take a good ten minutes' shuffling, too, before you got outside. Dad hated it.

I can only remember one occasion when the world of the screen and that of the audience became one. It was during the war, when there was a Deanna Durbin week at the Olympia, one of the local cinemas, but because of the snow that winter, the heaviest of all time (I know because I had a paper round) the roads were blocked, and the rolls of film couldn't be brought from Bolton. At the beginning of the performance, to our surprise, the lights went on, and the manager, a rather unusual man with a sissified voice and a broken nose like a boxer's, came on to the stage and told us that three lads had struggled waist-deep through the drifts across the moors to get the rolls there on time.

He ended, very cleverly, I thought, by saying, "I think I can fairly say that it was three smart boys who brought *Three Smart Girls*".

We clapped and clapped; and. somehow felt more involved in the film than we otherwise would have done. One of the three smart boys got bladder trouble, but it cleared up after a month or two.

I suppose there *could* have been other reasons why Dad would only sit on the end seat on the back row at the pictures, but for now these will have to do.

My Musical Education

When I were a lad we had no radio for many years, and pianos and that were only for people with brass. (We had a large zither with some broken strings, from long before my time but nobody ever played on it, or even told me what it was for.) But we were not without music.

For one thing, we had a little round tin wind-up gramophone with coloured pictures painted on the side.

We used to get it out on Saturday nights and have a musical evening while we were playing cards for toffees, but it had to be wound up after every song. To be quite truthful, I can only remember two, one was a crackly voice singing a song called "Revenge I cry!" and the other (it may even have been on the other side of "Revenge I cry!") was an even cracklier voice singing "On the Banks of Allan Waters" which is all I can remember of the words. It ended something like:

On the baanks of Alannn Waaaa-ters

Dee-dee-deedee - dee -dee (Crackle crackle)

One gramophone record might seem a bit minimal - this was before you could buy sixpenny Bing-singles at Woolies, but we had music in the house all day, because my Mother and for all I know my Dad as well had a bit of Welsh in them. I used to follow my Mother round the house while she dusted, or stirred the clothes in the dollytub with her possing stick, listening to old songs like *Soldiers of the Queen, Hold Your Hand Out You Naughty Boy, Goodbye Nellie Gray, The Rose of Tralee, All Through The Night* and (her favourite song*) Believe Me If All Those Endearing Young Charms:*

"For the heart that has truly loved, never forgets

But as truly loves on to the close;

As the sunflower turns on her God when he sets,

That same look which she turned when he rose."

all sung effortlessly in a big, clear, voice.

Dad like to sing too, strange old music-hall songs like:

"Ha Ha, Hee Hee

Cause Im not comin' back you see,

And if anybody knows a thing or two

It's me, me, me, me, me! "

Or *Yip-Aye-Yaddy-Aye-Yay, The Wibbly-Wobbly Walk, Show Me The Way To Go Home, Comrades, Get Yer 'air Cut,* and one haunting song about an old tramp, "like a bundle of rags come untied". "A bunch of young sportsmen came by" jeering at him, and he told them:

You may laugh, you may chaff,

Because I am down in the world;

But you'll find to your sor-row,

You're up today, and dahn to-morrow;

you can't put a stop to mis-for-tune,

For what has to be, will be;

And I may go up in the world like you,

An' you may come dahn like me..."

I wish I could remember more of that old song. I've never heard anybody else sing it. When Dad sang it, his

Lancashire voice unconsciously took on Cockney overtones ("dahn", "to-die") from his Chiswick boyhood at the turn of the century.

Dad used to pretend to do a kind of half-dance, sitting down and wobbling a knee:

"Hi-diddley-di-do,

Diddle diddle di-do

diddle diddle diddle doo da-day"

(He used the same melody to rock us to sleep on his knee). He told us that if he could just get the other leg going as well, we'd be well off. We used to watch, hoping he'd get the other one going and make us rich. In the meantime, you could try to win a toffee on Saturday night by singing *Tipperary* without laughing while he pulled funny faces. We never managed it (even Mother couldn't). But we got the toffees anyway.

My mother also used to sing strange Boer War songs, probably sung all over the country on 'Mafeking Night', like this one that went to the tune of *Rosie O' Grady*:

Lord Roberts and Kitchener,

Generals Buller and White

Baden-Powell and Macdonald

All ready to fight

And when the war's over

Oh, how happy we'll be

Marching into Pretoria,

General Buller and me

Another favourite was:

Goodbye Nelly I must leave you

Tho' it breaks my heart to go.

Something tells me I am needed

At the front to fight the foe;

See the soldier- boys are marching

And I can no longer stay,

Hark, the bugle-boys are calling,

Goodbye Nelly Grey!

While I was still on the right side of ten, we got hold of a square wooden gramophone which had probably had a big horn at one time before somebody threw it out. It had a very powerful spring and had to be wound up with what looked like an old-fashioned car handle. When the spring was wound tight (it could catch you a nasty crack over the fingers if it flew back) the only way to keep the spring coiled was to push the handle through a flatiron. It wasn't exactly fingertip technology, but it worked, and from somewhere we had got hold of a pile of records to continue our musical education.

I remember George Formby Senior "coughing better tonight" (I think he had TB.), Florrie Forde or Vesta Tilley or somebody like that, singing gloomy "jilted" songs like "There was I waiting at the church,":

"All at once, 'e sent along a note

'Ere's the very note

This is wot 'e wrote:

Can't get away

To marry you today -

My wife, won't let me."

and:

Her father turned up and her mother turned up

Her sister turned up and her brother turned up

Dear old Auntie Gert, poor old Uncle Bert

The parson in his long white shirt turned up;

But no bridegroom with a ring turned up,

Just a telegraph boy with his nose turned up,

With a telegram that read

He didn't want to wed

And they'd find him in the river with his toes turned up."

There was Billy Williams singing "When Father papered the parlour:"

Mother was stuck to the ceiling,

The kids were stuck to the floor;

I never saw a bloomin' family

So stuck up before...

We had Frank Crummett singing "Eleven More Months and Ten More Days" and "Abraham Lincoln Jones", Count John McCormack (I think he was a count of the Vatican or something) singing "By Killarney's Lakes and Fells,"; some Irish comic duo singing "A Jug of Punch"

"Wid a cherry pip-pin to cut an' crunch,

An' on the table, a jug of punch..."

and "Me Wooden McCarty", (about a widow who got somebody to model her dead husband from a chunk of wood and ended up in bed with the modeller) with its poignant conclusion:

"Says she,

"If ye're in want of a stick

Take a sloice out of Mick,

For Oi'm t'rough wid Me Wooden M'Carty!"

And for really serious listening, we had William McEwan singing *The Old Rugged Cross* and *We Will Talk It O'er Together By and By* . I hope they are. Talking it over together. And having a good laugh about it all.

Going to Blackpoo'

The furthest I ever travelled was to Blackpool, where we spent a week every year before the war.

The next furthest was with *Qantas* to Australia to see my mother, who was the first in the family with an Australian passport when she was about seventy. In Adelaide, she got as far as ninety-six, and loved everything about Australia except "barbies", because for some reason she didn't like her meat charred. Everybody except me left England when the Beatles arrived in 1962. I don't suppose that it was anything more than a coincidence, though.

I know I'm supposed to be writing about Blackpool, but I can't write about Blackpool without writing about my mother and dad. They were what it was all about, really.

There was an exciting, breathless week before we actually set off. Mother always bought us something new to go in, summer dresses for the girls, a new pair of navy-blue trousers for me, in the standard over-the-knee length. Whether that was the fashionable length or not, I don't know. I expect my idea of fashion was getting something new. There was all this air of bustle and washing and ironing and getting things ready for the off.

We always bought an enormous pap-mashay suitcase, big enough to carry the entire holiday wardrobes of five people, including spare shoes, and it always collapsed under the weight on the way to the station. Usually, the handle tore off at the bottom of Railway Road. It was an important part of the holiday ritual. It costs money to be poor. A leather suitcase or two would have saved many years' outlay, but who had leather suitcases in those days, except perhaps the people up Limes Avenue? And they didn't need to go to Blackpool. Jack Bury's mother who had a furniture shop on *The Green*, went to Ceylon, wherever that was. (On the big, tattered school map Owd Corran used to hang over the blackboard, it looked like something dripping off India.)

Limes Avenue were posh, weren't it! When I think about Limes Avenue, it seems to me to have been summer there forever, with stripes of sun and shadow all down the hill, and red and white striped canvas hanging in the doorways, like vanilla ice cream with raspberry vinegar, while a tired little boy limped past towards his tinned-salmon and lettice tea.

These suitcases we used to buy to go to Blackpool with were made of thin, shiny brown cardboard. They were big enough to carry a body in, about four feet long, three feet high and two feet wide. There were little brown tin triangles on the inner corners, and there were two locks, and keys on a piece of string. I suppose you might as well have put locks on a corn flakes packet for all the good they were, but they looked nice before they burst open. Our real defence against theft of course, apart from having a muscular Dad, was the fact that we hadn't anything worth stealing apart from the meat sandwiches, and my mother had those in a brown paper carrier bag with "Home and Colonial" written on the side.

On top of this huge case was a flimsy little tin handle which didn't leave much room underneath for Dad's thick fingers.

"Are we off then?"

The question always sent the excitement racing through me.

"Go on then, we're coming."

Mother always made the final round (she said) to see that everything was locked and barred and fastened in case anybody broke in and stole the family jewels.

My older sister Teresa waited for her, but my younger sister Margaret and I were already off with Dad down Johnny Wraith Brew, Dad carrying the huge case as carefully as he could in his big working-man's fist in case the tin handle tore off.

Holidays in those days were "staggered". Different towns - Bolton, Blackburn, Burnley and so on, went on holiday at different times or "wakes". For some reason which escapes me, my father used to go on holiday "Blackburn week" when everybody else in town was still at work, and as we went towards the station we met an endless stream of his workmates on their way to the factory.

Dad knew them all, and there was a sort of embarrassing royal progress through the middle of town.

"Playing you this week, Harry?"

"That's right, Will!"

"Nice day for gooin' off, eh Harry?"

"Very nice today, Tabby."

"Blackpool first stop, Harry?"

"We're hoping so, Tommy!"

And so on.

That was probably the real reason why my mother always lagged behind.

"Carry yer case, mister?"

Dirty face, ragged pants. It wasn't in my dad to say no, and the huge case would be turned over to a small boy, or more usually a couple of them, who would stagger with it for perhaps fifty to a hundred yards, progress gradually dwindling to a halt. Then Dad would take over again. At this point the handle would go, and he would hoist it on to a broad shoulder. The urchins, having done their bit and earned their tuppence, would straggle after us all the way up Railway Road to the station to be paid off.

Dad would buy the tickets. In the old, explosive days long before my time, when Blackpool had no slot machines, you made your own fun, mostly in the pubs. I heard that people took their food with them in big tin trunks- piles of sadcakes and legs of lamb and God only knows what, cowheels and trotters for all I know - and after paying their lodgings, they "spent up" every penny. If you'd had a really good week, all you had left the end of it was the return half of your ticket.

There would be hardly anybody waiting on the platform for the Blackburn train to come puffing out of the Sough Tunnel from Spring Vale. If you were only going to Blackburn, you went by tram. Over-excited, we crowded into one of the tiny compartments, our huge cardboard case already burst and buckled, and set off on the endless journey to the sea. I always sat opposite a little faded brown photograph of some hills called "Kyle of Lochalsh" where nobody had ever been.

Then Blackburn. All change. Blackburn was a real railway station, with a vast, dim roof full of echoes of hissing steam and thundering wheels. The platforms were alive with holidaymakers, stocky case-carrying Dads in caps and best suits, Mothers lugging in carrier bags and kids from the Boulevard, boys and girls with bare legs and sandals weighing themselves or coaxing penny bars of "Five Boys" chocolate or tiny packets of nuts-and-raisins out of the old red-painted cast-iron slot machines.

There was a long wait for the train to Preston. About a week out of a boy's life. And about another week (all change again) waiting *at* Preston. All really did change at Preston. It was completely foreign to us. You could easily tell a Blackburner of course. They talked a bit different,and their trams were different. But there was a certain likeness to us.

Preston was another world altogether. You could hardly understand a word they said. A man from Preston once came to our house. He let his raincoat trail into some real lemonade my mother had just made, and she threw it all out. Well, it just showed you.

That was all I knew about Preston then. To tell you the truth, I don't know much more now, though I once worked there for a few months. Very foreign, it was. The schools even played rugby.

My Dad changed at Preston, too. His face began to smooth out somehow, and smile more, as though he suddenly had something to laugh about. As he generally worked a hundred hours a week, I suppose he had.

He must have been looking forward to a rest. But he couldn't stop in bed, even at Blackpool. In those days workers got up all year at half-past five and clocked in at half-past six. When the holiday week came round, they would all be huddling on "the front" by seven, like silly beggars, out of sheer habit, waiting for the coffee stall to open. They used to tell one another, shamefaced, that they were "getting some ozone" before breakfast.

There was enough ozone for everybody at Blackpool. Layers of it.

On the last leg of the journey the train ran out of industrial Lancashire altogether on to the vast market-gardening steppes of the Fylde. From one horizon to the other, not a single mill-chimney, nothing but countless rows of cabbages and little garden huts and that. It was like crossing Siberia. It took at least another week, and you began to wonder whether the holiday wouldn't be over before you got there.

Then, suddenly, there were unmistakable signs of getting there. Sand dunes with rough grassy tops, windswept camping sites with rows of tiny "chalets" and one or two scruffy tents.

"That's Squire's Gate," Mother would tell us.

Squire's Gate...

A few sad bucket-carriers, leaning against the stiff breeze from the Irish Sea, would cross a camping site towards the ablutions. A small, blue-kneed boy or two would stand shivering and waving to the train. What were they doing out there, with Blackpool just down the line? Waving back, I could only think of one reason, probably the right one. They couldn't afford proper lodgings. Poor kids.

Then the enormous silver girders of the Big Dipper came into sight. And the Grand National switchback, where the year before, as everybody in Lancashire knew, somebody had fallen off and got killed.

We're at the South Shore! There, really there! And hooray, the sun's coming out as we roll into Central Station and join the queue pushing, mostly good naturedly, to get off the platform.

Down the incline, and along Chapel Street at the back of *Fairyland*, and the never-forgotten left turn into Oddfellow Street.

And there at the door, waiting for us, is Mrs Drabble herself. And her granddaughter Doreen. Mrs Drabble was a small, worried woman. Her husband on the other hand, was huge and loud and friendly, a bit like a Walt Disney giant. Somebody said he had been the first detective on the Blackpool police force, and you couldn't imagine any hankypanky going on in his house.

Our room was at the turn of the stairs on the right going up. It was always nice and clean, and full of beds. There were two big beds in it, anyway. Perhaps there were three, I can't remember, but you could run right round the room on them without touching the floor. And there was a jug-and-bowl-and-bucket corner.

There wasn't any bathroom, not for lodgers anyway. At any rate, I never saw one. I probably wouldn't have recognised a bathroom if I *had* seen one.

The lavatory was outside in the backyard, like ours at home; like all lavatories in those days, unless you were somebody like R.W.Holden who had a sausage factory. I'll tell you about our lavatory later. I might even tell you about R.W.Holden and what happened to Eleanor and Margaret Hargreaves's fingers there.

When my big sister Teresa got older, she still came to Blackpool. In fact she still came to Mrs Drabble's and shared a separate room with her girl friend Jean. Jean looked like Anna May Wong, or so people said. I didn't know who Anna May Wong was, but she must have been a bit on the skinny side and worn hornrimmed spectacles.

Mr and Mrs Drabble had had a large family with amazing names, as though the name Drabble wasn't amazing enough, names like "Ashforth". And to top it off, some of them had gone on the music-halls with an act called *The Four Elbards*, because "Elbard" is "Drabble" backwards; well, near enough.

The Drabbles had a chirpy granddaughter called Doreen. She was a bit on the skinny side, too, but pretty with dark hair and eyes. She overawed me a bit, because she lived at Blackpool, which put her in another world for a start. She (or perhaps her sister Olive) had been in a show at Blackpool Tower with Reginald Dixon at the *Wonder Wurlitzer*. And she supplied a sideshow on the *Golden Mile* with newts at ninepence apiece.

The Golden Mile, with Tussaud's and Luna Park and Fairyland as its main features, was a continuous line of ice-cream and catchpenny stalls down the front. Just north of the waxworks which apart from the *Chamber of Horrors*, contained "the sensational Liverpool Museum of Anatomy!" to goggle at, were the freak shows. Everything on the Golden Mile was sensational. It had to be, with the overheads the cheapjacks had to fork out.

Ex-Inspector Drabble knew them all. I suppose it was a bit ironic that his own granddaughter supplied them with newts.

The idea was simple enough. If you see a frog in a puddle, that's all it is, but if you see it in a sideshow in a big tank labelled "POISONOUS", you won't recognise it. Doreen's newts were advertised as MEXICAN AXOLOTLS, captured and imported at enormous expense.

The same sideshow had other astonishing creatures as well. Folk from Great Harwood, Chorley, Oswaldtwisle, poured in to goggle at "THE BUG DOG - HALF BUG, HALF DOG!" which turned out to be a little armadillo.

Another highly successful show some years later advertised ADOLF AND MUSSO, two GIANT RATS which had been blown out of the Liverpool sewers during the Blitz. They were actually two *coypus*, practically unknown in those days long before coypus overran Norfolk. Then there was the headless woman (with rubber pipes). I once paid to see "the mummified body of Jesse James," which looked like a lot of plaster painted brown, and probably was.

Most successful of all was ADAM. Jacob Epstein had made a rather odd sculpture of him with a sort of long, half-moon-shaped backward-leaning head, arms curled upwards, and *genitals*. Somebody had seen the possibilities of this, and much to Epstein's disgust, (he once told me about it) Adam was the sensation of the year on the Golden Mile with megaphones outside, bellowing "ARE YOU ASHIMED OF THE NIKED 'UMAN BODY?" and "TO THE PURE ALL THINGS ARE PURE!" and "WE DARE YOU TO SEE ADAM!"

They even had *SEPARATE SHOWINGS FOR MEN AND WOMEN,* in order to avoid embarrassment, like the Liverpool Museum of Anatomy at the waxworks just up the road. If that didn't fetch 'em in, nothing would. There were long queues of caps and headscarves all day at separate payboxes.

Perhaps the strangest character hanging round the Golden Mile in those days was *Stiffkey*. The name was good for a laugh in any pub, and came up frequently at the Drabbles' dinner table, but I was too young to appreciate the joke, or the one about seagull pies for that matter.

I gathered later that some clergyman from a place called Stiffkey had been unfrocked for immoral behaviour, and was now turning up in various sideshows on the Golden Mile including sitting in a cage with a lion.

For me, the best sideshow of all was a little booth on Central Pier where a demonstrator sold tricks like handkerchief into billiard ball, squirting cigarettes, stand-up playing cards, multiplying rings and double-bottomed drinking glasses. I used to stand there fascinated, listening to his patter over and over again like a favourite gramophone record. I expect he found me irritating, but I was never warned off, especially as I occasionally bought something, the handkerchief into billiard ball for example. I tried it, very clumsily, on Doreen, who saw immediately that the billiard ball was hollow. That was another reason why she overawed me a bit.

My Dad went to Blackpool to sit on the sands in the sunshine. That was *his* idea of a holiday. Margaret and I would trot across with him after breakfast, round the corner of Fairyland, with our buckets and spades, and he would choose a spot, always far enough on the north side of Central Pier to be well outside the shadow, and perhaps a hundred yards out from the prom. Everybody sat there. It was supposed to be cold on the other side of the pier.

And there, with our help, such as it was, he would shovel out a great hole with his big hands, slowly and enjoyably piling up the sand in a rampart all round, deep enough to sit in and big enough for half-a-dozen pairs of legs.(Blackpool, with an enormous beach of deep sand, covered twice a day by the sea, must be one of the few places in England where that can be done.)

Then he would settle back with a newspaper as the sun dried out the sand he had piled up, and by that time we would be fed up with digging, and our hands would be out for pennies. Ice cream cones cost a halfpenny or a penny, ice cream sandwiches twopence.

The sands were dotted with little ice cream stalls, pulled on by ponies, along with the Big Teapot, with a realistic spout and handle, which was rolled down on to the sands to sell jugs of tea, ham sandwiches and potato crisps.

There was a Punch and Judy show to end all Punch and Judy shows on the sands. "Professor Green" was famous all over the north, and so was "Dog Toby", a little white dog with a frill round its neck that used to sit on a shelf and join in the show, biting Punch and so on. I used to dream about having a little Dog Toby of my own. What I did eventually get was a brindle bull terrier called Cowboy who cheerfully went for everything in sight if he got out.

There were big open booths along the front where the trams rolled past to Bispham and Fleetwood. Both the booths and trams were packed with people. There was a mock auction where you gave two shillings - a lot, then- for a mystery parcel:

"Satisfied, are you, madam? *Are You Satisfied?* Tell them all...!"

Or you could watch them actually rolling enormous pink lengths of rock with the name *Blackpool* running right through it. Everybody took some sticks of rock home with them, even though it stuck to your false teeth. My Dad was always telling people he liked to suck a bit of rock in bed.

Another big open booth sold songs. I didn't know how you bought songs, - it was sheet music, I think - but I used to listen to them being sung, songs like:

Cowboy, you're a real humdinger

You're a hillybilly singer

*You're a **wow**, boy...*

and *Hands, Knees and Boomps-a-Daisy*, and *Amapola, My Pretty Little Poppy*, and

Little Sir Echo how do you do,

Hello, hello...

I suppose today's holidaymakers know more about Sirocco than Sir Echo.

A song I liked which sold well one year was:

Delia, Oh Delia

The Witch of the Wood...

which turned out to be Hitler's favourite song as well.

On Sundays, my crafty older sister used to join the Salvation Army, which rewarded the faithful with a halfpenny ice-cream cornet each, but she had to earn it. I was too young anyway, so I just watched.

The children were drawn up in lines along the prom, and learned strange songs with accompanying actions like:

Rolling over

Rolling over

My cup's full and rolling over,

Since the Lord saved me

I'm as happy as can be

My cup's full and rolling over.

There was also another one I rather liked, about a publican climbing up a tree, but all I can remember was the end:

"*And He said to him, "Zacchary, won't you please come down,*

'cause I'm coming to your house for tea."

Of course, I know now that publicans don't usually serve tea. Where you got a nice tea, with plaice and chips and a plate of bread and butter, as everybody in Lancashire knew, was at the U.C.P. somewhere near Hill's Bazaar. (U.C.P. stood for *United Cow Products*.) We sometimes had fish and chips in a little cafe at the back of Fairyland "for a change". It wasn't up to U.C.P. standards, though; there were eyes in the chips. There was a witty notice on the wall which said:

Our knives forks and glasses

My dear lads and lasses

Are not like doctor's medicine.

They are NOT TO BE TAKEN AFTER MEALS.

My mother would turn up on the sands an hour or two after we did. I thought it was because she was waiting until Dad had dug his big hole, but really it was because she went shopping every day. She bought our food and it was cooked for us at the lodgings. It came out cheaper that way.

She always knew exactly where to look for us, next to Central Pier. And so did Mr and Mrs Bradshaw and little Hilda from the next street at home, Mr and Mrs Elliott, Eric and Dorothy from Sheffield, and others. It has only just struck me as odd, looking back, that Dad used to sit there in the sunshine wearing a full navy-blue serge outfit, including the waistcoat, and never so much as took his jacket off. I don't think he even took off his collar or tie. The only concession he made to sunbathing was removing his cap for a limited period. Within an hour or two, his face would go brick red, his forehead would start to peel, and everybody would comment on it. " Ee, Harry, you do catch the sun, don't you!"

"Ee, yes, he picks up a tan like nobody's business, does Harry."

Dad was rather proud of his ability to pick up a quick tan, though it never got further down than his collar. Having a red face was proof both that you had been to Blackpool and that, as always, it had done you a world of good. Somebody commiserating with a neighbour who had recently lost her husband, got the reply, "Yes, it was very sad. We'd just been to Blackpool, too, and you know, it had done him a world of good."

Paddling along the edge of the sea was an important part of the holiday. Mother would tuck her frock inside her knickers, Dad would take off his shoes and socks and roll his trousers up to just under the knee, and we would join the multitudes, watching the waves creaming up our calves. There were fascinating pools round the huge iron legs of the pier, much deeper than they looked. Sometimes there were jellyfish and strange little efts swimming about in them. I had been warned to keep away from them, but one day the inevitable happened and I fell into one of the pools.

I can still remember the water closing over my head as I went down. You were supposed to come up three times before you drowned, but I only remember kicking and thrashing about and swallowing gallons of sea water.

I still don't know how my Dad got there in time, but he did. He must have covered the hundred yards or so to the pool like a Derby winner. I suppose I owe my life to the fact that he wasn't a bank manager. He plunged straight in, blue serge suit and all, and pulled me out gurgling and spluttering.

I got my legs smacked by my mother all the way back to Mrs Drabble's for ruining Dad's new suit. He had to walk back with us, dripping, all the way past the Brunswick. There were men on the steps he knew, some with early pints enjoying the passing parade.

"Been having a bit of a paddle, Harry?"

"You are *Lobby Ludd*, and I claim the five-pound prize!"

Dad nodded gamely and squelched grimly onward towards his change of clothes, sports coat, flannels, and "monk shoes".'

We used to go back to Mrs Drabble's for tea. You had to be back in time for three meals a day, and it generally meant a rush, shaking off the sand, collecting buckets and spades, taking back the jugs and cups to the Teapot, carrying the deckchairs back to get your deposit, and so on. After tea, we might be left upstairs in bed with comics and lucky bags, but we were only there for the week, and were usually outside again when the lights came on and the wind got up.

There were evening "mystery tours" on a "chara". They usually ended up at the *Welcome Inn*, where children, unwelcomed and unlicensed, sat outside with a bag of Smith's Crisps in a damp smell of malt to the sound of clinking glasses and a lot of shouting and laughing. The story got round that one party went on a mystery tour and were taken back home to Sunnyhurst Wood.

I used to get ten shillings pocket money for the week, though Dad was always good for more if you wanted badly to buy something like a handkerchief -into – billiard- ball, or an ice-cream cone. I even coaxed him into buying me a big black pocketknife, but after I had managed to gash myself with it a few times it disappeared.

"I've rubbed all the skin off the back of my bloody hand getting money out of my pocket for thee" he used to grumble. My mother used to see to it that we started slowly and still had something to spend on the South Shore later in the week. I remember Dad taking me to see the famous laughing clown in a big glass case in front of the Fun House. It sort of wriggled and writhed to the sound of wild recorded laughter.

"You can't keep your face straight," he told me, "You can't help but laugh yourself." I thought it was interesting, but I didn't laugh, and he told me I had no sense of humour.

Still, he did buy a couple of tickets for us for the Fun House, and we went past the pay box, sat on two little rugs on a moving platform, and started to rise upwards. We were about fifty feet up, looking down on the Fun House roof, before Dad began to suspect that there was "summat wrang." We rose still higher in the air until we could see the whole of the South Shore spread out below us, and suddenly a man dashed out from a sort of hole, as I remember it, grabbed the back of Dad's rug and dragged it from under him.

"Here! What the bl...!" was all he had time for, before he was whizzing downwards, round and round, on the long shining slide of the Jack and Jill, with me a-following after. He was still swearing when he reached the bottom, but I don't think he got his money back.

At the beginning of one Blackpool holiday, retired Detective-Inspector Drabble, who was now a beekeeper for a solicitor called Woosnam, generously presented my father and Ernie, my cousin's Mary Ann's husband, with a pile of "workclothes".

We watched them solemnly climb *together* into an enormous pair of pants and don an enormous shirt, an arm apiece in each sleeve, and stumble round the room. It was better than Doodles at the Tower Circus. They had to get rid of the clothes without hurting Mr. Drabble's feelings, and it turned into a competition between the two of them which became a family legend.

Ernie started the contest by taking a boxful of the clothes to a photographer's and telling one of the assistants that somebody had asked for them as props for outsize customers. He came back grinning, empty-handed.

My father trumped this as only he could have done, by walking up to the ticket-window at Blackpool Tower and stuffing a large pair of checked trousers through the hole, with the barefaced assertion: "Jack towd me to leave these here!"

When the girl inside actually began to pull the trousers into the box, my mother, fearfully half-watching from the distance, had to go out on the promenade for a great whiff of ozone. By the time she had recovered, my father had half-filled the paybox with huge jackets and trousers and made his escape.

The week ended with a kind of smash-and-grab raid in reverse when Ernie opened the side door to a shop, flung in an enormous suit and took to his heels; and with the ritual burying in the sand of the final article of clothing, a raincoat-for-two.

Olympia was one of the places I was taken to in the evening, and with its shows and booths and stalls, I liked it almost as much as the Tower Circus. I remember going to little shows there, one by a group of Icelanders, all with white hair and pink eyes, dressed in high boots and big jerseys and another by Africans in grass skirts and monkey-tails. Somewhere about the house is a little black bean I bought from the Africans as a good luck charm. In one of the booths selling cosmetics a demonstrator made up my cousin Mary Ann, who was small with black hair and brown eyes, as an elegant Japanese lady (with a Lancashire accent). Ernie, her husband, an ex-boxer and gardener, looked embarrassed to me, but my mother and sister said they could tell he was pleased. In another year or two he would be a maritime gunner, adrift in an open boat for three days after being torpedoed, but none of us could tell that.

I remember Darwen's chief celebrity Bill Hunt in the final Tower Circus water scene, covered with gold. It was Dad who told me he'd originally come from Darwen. "That's that Bill Hunt! Used to do handstands on the back of park benches while we were dragging machines around at work."

The last time I was in Blackpool a few years ago, I went back to Olympia to look for the Icelanders and the Japanese lady stall, but all I found was an endless, dreary row of one-armed bandits.

My Bike George

After acting up for a week or two (crying and that). I finally got a new *bike* for six pounds fifteen from a shop down Blackburn Road (Duckworth Street?) that took my Dad months to pay off at five shillings a week, a *new Hercules* with a seagull or a dove or something on the front badge and the word BRINDIA, but I couldn't call it BRINDIA, could I, so I called it George after a popular radio figure's bike.

The radio cyclist also recommended cyclists to carry a water pistol full of ammonia to deal with angry dogs. That was one thing I didn't copy. I mean, even if you could afford it all, where would you keep your ammonia pistol? In a holster on the handlebars? Anyway, there were dogs and their offerings of every shape and size everywhere when I were a lad. It was like a law of nature, if you left them alone, they left you alone. As far as I can remember, I was never attacked by dogs apart from Billy Marsden of course (we named dogs after their owners then). All the Marsdens were like that, humans and dogs, except Arthur Marsden, who owned his own house and was on the Council.

Oh, and there was a big black and white spaniel called Kim Bellman that kept trying to mate with my leg on the way to school. It got to be a right nuisance, shouting for Eleanor to come out and get Kim off, but at least it was trying to be friendly, I suppose.

Bicycle clips. That's something else you don't see much of nowadays. No comic patter on the wireless was complete then without a joke about bicycle clips. I didn't need them when I got my bike because in those days, like other lads just getting into their teens, I wore short pants and long stockings with turned-down tops and garters. Actually, the pants weren't all that short, they came down to your knees. I once heard somebody in a shop call them "boy's knickers". I didn't like that. You kept them up with braces, or in summer with a red-and-white striped elastic belt from Woolworth's with a snake-shaped buckle at the front. I didn't start to write about clothes, though, but about bicycles. When I did finally get my first suit with long pants, I already had George and needed the clips. They didn't keep all the black oil off my trouser cuffs, but as they were dark blue serge it didn't show much.

I have never owned another *new* bicycle, though I've ridden a few. My Dad taught me how to ride by telling me what would happen if I fell off. Wibble wobble.

"Thee fall off! That's all! Tha'll see!"

We started off in a field with Dad holding the back of the seat and pushing ("Pedal, can't you! What do you think the bl**dy pedals are for?") and I remember finally trundling down Sunnyhurst Road with Dad's voice getting fainter in the distance until I fell off again because I didn't know how to turn or to use the brakes. But at least, now I was on the way. I hated my dad's cycling lessons - "Thee fall off! That's all!" But he mended it for me, leaving the mark of clamps on the handlebars I ha foolishly taken off to turn upwards.

George had no gears and I rather envied kids who had them on. I tried "fixed gear" (Turning the wheel round. I hadn't realised I'd have to pedal all the time (no freewheel) and got my shins bruised when my foot slipped off on a downhill.

As you cycled down Blackburn Road, past the Boundary and down the Cravens -a steep, cobbled, treelined hill, the others came out of side streets and joined the Darwen gang. Bicycling to school in Blackburn, with Tommy Duckworth, Raymond "Dink" Hill, Wolfish Bulcock, Flash Donnelly, Ken Walsh on wooden rims, and Vin Humphries whose bike had stuck permanently in high gear.

The tramlines in places, Ewood was worst, were only a few inches from the curb. You could get crushed, pedalling furiously through Ewood with the tram clinking a sort of bell behind you. There was one long sweep up Preston New Road where the tram driver used to leave his brass handle at the front and sit on the back step having a smoke. It frightened non-Blackburners to death.

I remember my Blackpool 'adventure', falling on the wet and muddy road after church. Falling off George after Mass in front of the Olympia cinema one Sunday morning in my brand new blue serge suit with long pants, I got them all muddy. I daren't go home so I set off and cycled all the way to Blackpool and back. Thirty miles! When I got back I just brushed my knees at the door and Glory be, all the mud just fell off – it had dried to dust!

Today I'd have been run over, but then, there were hardly any cars - but I remember one accident, well, as a sudden thump on the way down East Park Road when my cycling companion vanished. He'd run into a car door as it opened.

The bike shed at school was full. I remember admiring Edgar Bolton's *Rudge Whitworth* with its short handlebars, and I remember bicycling over Bull Hill to Bolton and Radcliffe, no sound but the swish of types on the tar macadam - unusual and wonderful in an age of cobblestones, over Dunscar and nearly all the way to Bolton.

There were runners along the roads even then. Possibly practicing for the famous *Playing fields to Darwen Tower race* .

The race normally involved running from Sett End (Hoddlesden) paling fields down the Roman Road, and then either over the Jerry Tops or Sudell Road and Red Earth Road down the steps into Sunny Bank Street, through the Olympia entry, up Johnny Wraith Broo, up Beckett Street and across to Punstock or through Bold Venture Park, round the Lickle Toffee Shop to the Agnozzery, and then up the moors to the Tower. The runners were clocked in at the Tower and then back to Sett End. It was open only to Darreners

I don't remember whether the race was *initiated* during the George V Silver Jubilee celebrations, but I remember the big rivalry on that occasion: Wally Parks versus Johnny Laver. The reason I remember is because Parks was given a walkover victory when Johnny Laver was found to have used public bus transport

Picknicking

All I have to do is to bite into a tinned salmon sandwich. Even *tuna* will do it. And there I am, setting off again on foot for the Playing Fields at Blacksnape up on the other side of the valley.

I knew our side, a higher, steeper one, or some of it anyway, but the other side was unknown. Going across was a special adventure.

Those Western movies showing a group of pioneers winding down into Indian territory with their pack horses, remind me of our little band going down Mill Gap, following the big redbrick
wall of the paper mill and starting up Ball Street Broo, me in front, scouting, Margaret in the middle and my mother fetching up the rear with her brown paper carrier bag with Home and Colonial on it.

My mother used to make three kinds of sandwiches, salmon, tomato, and salmon and tomato. They all tasted very different, but I can't remember which I liked best. The tomatoes had a stronger flavour than they have now, and the tinned salmon was redder. Whether that was because it was better or worse than it is now, I don't know. The same applies to me, for that matter.

The sandwiches were made with "Veget", sliced white loaf, and were well seasoned with salt and pepper. Usually, by the time we got round to eating them, some of them had got a bit squashed. Perhaps that gave them an extra bit of flavour. Along with the sandwiches, Mother would take a paper bag with tea and sugar. I don't think anybody drank their tea without sugar in those days.

The mixture was called a "brewin'", which reminded me of bears."Are you takin' a bruin?" or "Don't forget to take your bruin," always had this special echo for me. I always felt that little bit safer when we had a bruin with us, hulking along at the back. Not that we really needed him.

Nothing could go wrong when my Mother was there. She was a sturdy woman, and well over five feet in height. On my way to school, a big dog called Billy Marsden used to rush out at me suddenly through a gate, but not when my Mother was there or when we had a bruin with us. And of course, with your bruin there was always a little bottle of milk with a cork which smelled a bit sour even after it had been boiled, so some people just used a wad of paper. Not toilet paper, because most ordinary people didn't buy it in those days. They used newspaper. We used to use the Radio Times, though we had no radio, but the Smiths next door (our landlords) used the same lavatory as we did and hung up their weekly Radio Times on a nail.

We only went to the playing fields when it was a hot day, and it was a long way to walk. It was the long slow, walk that made it so special. There were no cars at all, and the streets were quiet and empty. We walked through great patches of shadow thrown by the high factory walls, cool, narrow back streets, and there was a long hard sunny climb up alongside the paper mill wall.

We used to come out into a long avenue where people were better off. There were red and white striped canvas awnings covering the open doorways. Queer little garden gnomes stood among the flowerbeds. And at the end of the avenue, at last, there was the great cool arch of trees over a lane flanked with hen-pens, and you came out of the lane beside a long row of tiny, freshly painted miners' cottages and saw the open country across the Roman Road.

From there it was just a walk across the fields and a struggle through a couple of stiles to get to the bottom end of the playing fields, which weren't at all what you would expect. They covered an enormous area which has probably been built up long before. The upper end, probably opened by the Prince of Wales or somebody like that, had swings and roundabouts and rocking horses and a big and rather frightening helter-skelter. The lower end was a great sloping field with strange little clumps of trees and widely separated groups of high-backed seats of brownish stone. There was a stone table to put the tomato sandwiches on and the jug of hot water and the cups my mother went for. When you sat on the seat you couldn't reach the table. I couldn't, anyway. And you couldn't pull up your chair, either. And your feet dangled over the muddy ground.

There was no pop or orange squash. The only thing squashed was the tomato sandwiches, and you had a cup of milky, sugary tea with them. And then it was soon time to start on the long walk home, the long shadows keeping up with our tired legs all the way up Mill Gap and Spring Gardens, Mother in front now, but not too far.

The Osram Music Magnet

When I were a lad, we had gaslight. (I was born just too late for candles or storm lanterns.) Instead of electric light bulbs, we had to buy gas mantles, little white beehives that you fitted on upside down over the gas jet in the middle of the ceiling. They were very thin and you had to be careful not to put your fingers through them, so I wasn't allowed to touch them. I can still remember how when my Dad held a lit match to the mantle after it had been fitted and turned on the gas, the whole room was suddenly flooded with light and the mantle shone down through the clothes rack like a little sun. You could hear the gas if you were very quiet, but it wasn't really worth it.

The best thing about having been brought up with gaslight though, was that it made it so exciting when we got electric light instead! It put sixpence a week extra on our rent, (one-and-ninepence the rent was) but *I* didn't have to go without Holland toffee to pay it, and I stood there switching the bare bulb on and off and on again until my mother couldn't stand it anymore and told me to stop before I wore out the switch. It's only when you don't take something for granted that you can get really excited about it. If you were born with a family car, or began to fly when you were two years old, it doesn't mean the same to you as it does to somebody who has to wait for it. Even if you never get it.

I can still remember the thrill - and that is the right word, I think - of getting a wireless. I came home from school one afternoon, and there in the corner, fastened high up on the wall beyond my reach, was a square, shiny brown box with a little knob on the side.

It was a "relay", I was told, and that meant that we had a speaker but no actual wireless set. It also meant for some reason that we could only listen to the "National" and not to the "Regional" programme. Much I cared. We had God's plenty right in the house with us now.

I was just about the right age for *Children's Hour*, for Auntie Doris, Auntie Violet and Uncle Mac taking us for walks in the country, bird-watching and talking to farmers, and their dog Raq chasing rabbits.

"Just look over there, Violet, in the corner of the field! Don't move. Keep hold of Raq..."

"Oh, yes, I see it! It's lovely! What is it?"

"It's a wood pigeon."

"Wuff! Wuff!"

"Oh, look, it's flown away!"

I wonder who did the wuffing. Auntie Violet, perhaps.

And *Toytown*, with Larry the Lamb ("Oh, Mister Maaaaayor sir!") and (my Dad's special favourite) Dennis the Dachshund with his gruff voice: ("Dot vos goot, Larry!) .

I remember running home in the rain up Spring Gardens to listen to the next instalment of "The Lost World", or Howard Marshall reading *Brother Blackfo*ot. I remember afternoons listening to Howard Matrshall's deep, dark blue, reassuring voice (I pictured him as a sort of plain-clothes policeman with a bowler hat and a big black moustache) at Test Matches:

"Bradman rolls the ball back along the carpet, and that's the end of the over."

And there was *At The Black Dog*, and *In Town Tonight* "stopping the roar of London's traffic", and Henry Hall, who used to say, "Good evening! This *is* Henry Hall's Guest Night" in case you might perhaps think it wasn't... and *Monday Night at Seven* with Arthur Askey, and Inspector Hornleigh and Sid Walker and *Palace of Varieties* with Nosmo King and Harry Hemsley and the Vagabond King and Billy Bennett ("almost a gentleman").

In the middle of the war, our landlord who owned the off-licence next door, asked us to move from number twenty-six to number twenty at the end of the row to make room for some of his family. We carried our furniture down the back street at night. Mother said it must have been the gipsy in us. As we now had a flimsy, tarred "gable end" directly exposed to bombing, a hundred yards or so from one of the biggest munitions factories in the north, it wasn't the most sensible thing we ever did. Dad reinforced the coal shed next to the lavatory with concrete and sandbags as an air-raid shelter. Luckily our narrow back street was overshadowed by a towering wall of stone blocks which would have put any ancient castle to shame.

Still, we did finally get our very own wireless set, left behind by 'Becca and Susie, the two old ladies who moved out somewhere else. It was an *Osram Music Magnet*. Even in those days, it must have been a relic, probably the only one left in the world. It was, like, a long box with a kind of grey pebble-ash finish. It stood on top of a big cabinet with glass doors. Inside the cabinet, behind two green old-maidy curtains, was all the innards, miles of wire, valves, the wet battery and so on. If you folded back the hinged lid of the long grey box, (I had to stand on a chair to do it) you looked down on two sections, each holding a sort of black metal cylinder about the size and shape of a toilet roll stood on end.

A metal rod stuck out of the centre of each one, ending in a little coloured knob, one blue and one red. If you pushed the blue one down, you were supposed to get the National programme, and if you pushed the red one down, you got the Regional programme, or so my Dad said. It must have been an early way of tuning in. As a matter of fact, if you pushed either of them down, you got an electric shock. I tried it, so I know. It made no difference to the programme as far as I remember. I don't think I ever heard "Regional" at all, if there was any.

But we heard Owd Churchill on it on Sunday nights. For all his 'rhetorical genius', we found Churchill to be mainly enigmatic in his wartime 'Sunday Broadcasts'.

"Aye, well, we're on our way to them there 'sunny uplands' according to Churchill."

"What were that about 'sunny uplands'?"

"Damned if I know.."

And of course, the famous broadcast after El Alamein:

"Now this is not the end. It is not even the beginning of the end. But it is, perhaps, the end of the beginning. *Goodnight.*"

We just sat staring at one another, then Dad said:

"E's at it again, i'n't 'e?"

We heard Terence de Marney doing the *Count of Monte Christo* and *The Cloister and the Hearth*.

Every so often I would come home and find Dad with the whole thing disemboweled on the table, holding the ends of spluttering wires against various bits of metal. If you knew what was good for you, you made a bolt for it, but you usually ended up holding a bit of wire while Dad puzzled over it. His skin must have been like an electrician's gloves, and he had to use us to test for current.

"Just ged owd o' that bit o' blue wire over there, will you?"

"Oh, no Dad! I don't want to!"

"GED OWD OF IT!"

"Oooowwww! Ooooowww! I got a shock! I got a shock!"

Dad would shake his head judgmatically and perhaps scratch it, muttering to himself.

"Aye, well. T'current's comin' through *theer* then..."

But the worst job was going right up Bolton Road to Malkin's wireless shop- about half-an-hour's walk - to get the "wet battery" charged. It was a sort of oblong glass container weighing a couple of pounds with a handle on a frame. We used two, one being charged and one in use. The charge lasted a few days. I didn't like Malkin. As far as I know, nobody did.

"Just goo up to Malkin's with this battery and get it charged, will you? And be careful how you carry it.

Don't drip any of that acid on your legs, or it'll burn you."

I'd to try to hold the thing out away from my legs going along the road, but it was too heavy for that, and I used to creep round the long bend past Saint Joseph's School like somebody carrying a live hand grenade, with my long grey woollen stockings pulled up over my knees. I never got any acid burns, but I can remember that on my school report it once said "He is inclined to be nervous".

No bloody wonder.

We took the little square speaker with us from number twenty-six. It stood next to the Osram Music Magnet on an old cast-iron sewing machine. The sewing machine weighed a ton and had a sort of lacy cover thrown over it. I never saw anybody use it, and I expect it was broken. I suppose I took it for granted that it was a natural part of the furniture, though it was about the only thing "us Dad" hadn't made himself. I don't know what would have happened if we had chucked it out. It would just have had to stand in the back yard somewhere, because the ash-tub men wouldn't have taken it. Even Dad must have found it heavy, carrying it from number twenty "on his hump", as Mother used to say, though he always carried himself as straight as a guardsman.

Once when I was ill, Dad somehow managed to put another old speaker, a sort of big round silvery metal thing that he'd scrounged from somewhere, upstairs at the side of my bed, so I could listen to *The Gang Smasher*: ("Dees ees Tor-toni....You 'ave blundered again, Meester Gang-Smasher!" Ha Ha Ha!), and one morning , I could hear my Mother and our Margaret, through the speaker, talking in the house downstairs. I shouted "Mother!" and I heard her say "Ee! Listen, love. That's our Arthur on the wireless!"

It was, like, a blooming miracle. I had Tortoni, and Marconi as well. I could shout "Mother, can I have something to drink?"

"Yes, love, what would you like?"

"Have you any sasparella?"

"I'll just have a look...."

It's a funny world. I can remember threepenny bits. They even made some posh thick ones with about twelve sides and a robin on one side and a thistle on the other. I remember when you could get Bing Crosby records at Woolworth's for sixpence. Now, not only is there no Bing, No Woollies and no sixpences, but there's no records either.

Yes, I *have* got a telly now, as though you might think perhaps I hadn't. I even have a telephone. For me, they haven't got what that old speaker upstairs had got. But I expect that's because I had something then that I haven't got any more.

The Landmine

At the end of the row we lived in was some "spare land" that was what was left after a factory fire disaster before I was born. The remains of the burned factory had been thrown into the old "mill lodge".

When I was a little boy it was almost like a rough park, a riot of brushwood and butterflies and big yellow dandelions and huge flat stones the girls played at chopping on.

You couldn't play with a ball there but it was a popular children's playground. We called it the Top.

At the other side of the Top was the new factory, an enormous wall of bright red brick that seemed to me to go up into the sky. The only thing higher was the black mill chimney towering over the wall. I once saw my Dad walk round the top of the wall and climb the chimney, stopping every so often to put his leg through the rungs and give his hands a rest. Workmen in those days had to have hands like clamps, and no nerves. Once at the top of Blackpool Tower, he hung upside down over the wooden barrier and wrote our names there in pencil, five hundred feet in the air.

The factory had gone over to making munitions. Jerry was after it all right. So, the area was *likely* to be bombed. Getting under the stairs when the big chimney blew - (that's what I thought the siren was) made sense because we were in the middle of a row of solid little limestone grit houses with a great black wall towering behind them, like a castle wall but thicker. Still, my Dad wasn't satisfied until he found something safer.

What he found was an old, abandoned farmhouse up on the moors he could rent for a couple of shillings a week. It was known locally as Clambelly Farm. Dad told me that it called that because the farmer used to give his kids tuppence to go without any supper, and then charge them tuppence for their breakfasts, but I couldn't see them falling for that more than once, unless they were potty, which wasn't altogether unlikely living in a place like that.

One night when the moonlight made it almost like daytime outside, the big chimney blew, and Dad said, right, get your coats on.

Mother had a long white nightdress on under her overcoat, and Dad went on ahead to start a fire. The town sloped up to the moors and we were climbing all the time, up past the Coop and round the Park, where the great iron fence had gone for scrap, up past Mr Kershaw's - our milkman's - field at the bottom of the moors, winding up on the stony path past the Little Toffee Shop where you had to bend down to a cellar window to buy your caramels, the big blackberry bushes, and the cricket field with the beams of searchlights swinging across the night sky looking for Jerry.

The furniture at Clambelly Farm was an old twenty-foot-long school bench Dad had dragged inside. It was used for sitting on, on the cricket field. We sat there shivering waiting for the fire Dad had made of odds and ends of wood, to "gate up", and after a while I managed to slip outside on to the big level field. The town could be seen plainly, the searchlights were flashing round, and great flares hung in the sky. There was a distant thunder of guns. Then I was marched firmly inside and settled on the worn wooden bench where so many other little backsides had squirmed. There was nowt to eat or drink. Not even a cup of tea.

I think it was that that decided my Mother against Clambelly Farm, and the next outing was to Auntie May Whittaker's, up Redearth on the other side of the valley and away from bomber targets. Auntie May was the only one of my father's sisters who looked at all like him. For some reason the boys had big conks and the sisters little oriental turned-up noses. Auntie May Whittaker had a conk and a big pile of white hair. There was a picture of my grown-up cousin Tim in a kind of navy lieutenant's uniform on the sideboard and a concertina in a box that Uncle Dick could play (a bit). It was dull at Auntie May's but we did get to sleep. The only bit of excitement I remember was who pee-ed the bed. Auntie May accused me, but Mother was indignant and said it was probably Tim.

Whether it was because of some such argument or not I don't know, but we set off back home about midnight. The All Clear had gone, there was a full moon, and we wended our weary way down Sudell Road, through Sunny Bank Street and the Olympia entry, up Johnny Wraith Broo, and stumbled into bed, Margaret and Mother in the front bedroom, Dad and me in the back one. My single bed was a bit exposed over by the window, and I slept in the bigger one with my Dad.

We got undressed and into bed, quite unaware that we were the only people left in the district. A German landmine had fallen at the top of nearby Alice Street and the area had been evacuated by the air raid wardens. They were supposed to be on guard, but we had gone past without being noticed.

About three in the morning, the heavens opened. There was a deafening roar and I woke up in a cloud of dust and smoke.

As the landmine went off, Dad threw himself over me, but apart from black faces we were both unhurt. Part of the roof had fallen in, and my little bed was crushed under broken beams and slates.

We pushed our way out on to the landing, where we met Mother. When she saw our black masks she started screaming until Dad told her to pipe down. She said she thought it was blood. It wasn't, but it must have been a shock, and it didn't make things any better when the Smiths, who owned the off-licence next door asked us to move.

Like most working-class families then, we only rented the house, and our landlords the Smiths wanted it for their son or daughter and family. So we moved in the middle of the war from number 26, to number 20, the end house of the row, doing a flit in the dark, carrying everything round the back over the wet, slippery cobblestones. One of the Mrs Smiths complained later that they took about half-a-dozen layers of wallpaper off the walls; Mother was up in arms about that, but Dad just said that if they had taken that much paper off, the bloody walls would have collapsed.

There wasn't much difference inside the houses, but whilst number 26 was snugly buried in the middle of the row, number 20 had a tarred black "gable end" wall made of boarding and roofing material.

It would have been about as much protection against a bomb blast as a Home and Colonial carrier bag, so Dad got to work on the coalhole.

Every house in the row had a little stone split-level backyard. At the top of the yard was the lavatory and a sturdy brick outhouse used for coal. Dad reinforced the top with iron bars and thick concrete, and built a double wall of sandbags in front of the outhouse. Behind it was a narrow back street and this enormous wall made of great blocks of stone.

When the siren went, we would troop up the yard and sit on the bench Dad put inside, peering up through the half-open door at the black bulk of the roof outlined against the moonlit sky. Mother insisted that she could tell a German aeroplane engine:

"I can hear them prowling round...they're up there somewhere."

Wrapped up in blankets, Margaret and I would nod off, and waken up to the smell of egg-and-bacon wafting through the back-kitchen window. Our Teresa worked on munitions at the Fuse Factory, and when she wasn't on firewatching duty there she would come home at all hours.

Mother used to shout to her to come into the shelter but she wasn't having any. She sat there in her overalls, polishing off an early breakfast and ignoring all Mother's dire warnings ("You'll know about it one of these days!") while our noses twitched hungrily.

Sometimes Dad was there. It was better then. Safer. But sometimes he was out in the blitz with a big elephant's-trunk gas mask and a fire-axe. The factory fire brigade had been organised to protect the factory, but Dad and his workmates came home tired out from firefighting in Manchester and Liverpool. Mr Turner across the street was over age for the army, but he joined an anti-aircraft group to defend the district, and his wife and kids never saw him again for about six years. Where he got to, I don't know, but little Harry Turner once came outside with a fez on.

The Chip Butty

It seems a bit funny writing about chip butties on a computer and seeing it all come up on a seventeen-inch screen. When I was born (not all that long ago – I still have my hair and teeth) we had no electric light, no wireless, in fact nowt, really.

My mother boiled water on a sort of "hob" that swung out over the fire in a big, blackened pan with a steel bobber in it. The bobber was to stop it from getting all orange inside with rust, only it didn't work. And she made our dinners in a big iron oven next to the fire and had to keep pushing red-hot coals underneath it all the time to keep it hot. It sounds a bit odd, today, and I suppose that nobody with all their chairs at home would go in for it nowadays. But that's what it was like for everybody then who didn't go to pictures with Tom Walls and Ralph Lynn in them and did go to pictures with Jimmy Cagney or George Formby. Only, if you were on the dole, bringing up a family on twenty-six shillings a week, you didn't go to the pictures at all, not even the tuppeny laugh-and-scratch. And you didn't have any reason to warm your oven.

No, if you wanted a hot dinner with a bit of entertainment thrown in, - and who didn't?- you went to the chip shop. Chip shops did more to keep things going than anything. More than Ramsay Macdonald and Stanley Baldwin and all that lot put together. A lot of people thought it was Baldwin who should have abdicated instead of Eddie. And it wasn't Ramsay Macdonald that was the *Boneless Wonder*, either. It was the fish and chip dinner.

A chip butty doesn't sound like much to write home about nowadays, four warm chips – or five on the whopper version, squashed in melting margarine between two thin slices of bread. But compared with the other kinds of portable butty available , it was pretty near the top of the list. Jam butties of different kinds, including the treacle butty and the syrup butty, did seem to me to be worth running in to your Mum for. But not sugar butties, popular with little girls, or mustard butties; or , if you were on the dole, a chipless *salt-and-vinegar* butty . I expect I was a bit spoiled.

On my way home from the pictures in Leeds a few years ago, I thought that, for once anyway, I'd take home a fish-and-chip supper. When I unwrapped them, they were absolutely ghastly. A soggy mess. I don't need to go into detail, it's happened to you. The interesting thing is that they could get away with it. I suppose in a town the size of Leeds there's always somebody popping in to be caught napping, somebody who hasn't been there before and who won't be going back. Like me.

When I were a lad, folk would walk miles to find a *gradely* chip shop. If your chips and fish weren't good, you'd have been out of business in a week. The word spread quick in those days, and there was always a queue at *Crompton's* where my mother used to send me for three fours o' chips to go with the gurnards she bought "under t'Glass Shed". The chips were golden brown and crisp enough to survive being carried home wrapped first in wrapping paper and then in newspaper in a bundle that warmed all your arm by the time you got home.

Crompton's was a small, crowded, but clean, take-away, where the main entertainment feature was the chip-slicer, a sort of guillotine that turned potatoes into raw chips in front of your very eyes. Whenever I go to see a French Revolution picture, I still find myself unconsciously searching the cast for small, dark Mr. Crompton. The other chief entertainment feature was the rhythmic banging of the metal basket on the edge of the hissing vat which meant that another batch of chips was ready, perhaps even yours. Mrs Crompton, a tall, pale bespectacled lady, scientifically measured your fourpennyworths with her scoop . I don't know if she actually counted the chips, or if just looked as though she did. Then on with the newspaper, and down home you went as fast as your little legs could carry you. I used to wonder why Mrs Crompton was about a foot taller than Mr. Crompton, but if I asked my mother about things like that, she just used to say "As God made them, He paired them."

Crompton's was handiest for us, but there was a very popular chip-shop on the main road at the bottom of Radford which was a lot more entertaining. For one thing, the lady behind. the counter was my ten-year-old idea of beautiful, with long dark hair (not really very practical over a big vat of red-hot fat,) and a fascinating moustache. And in the window, there was a great big picture of the Devil looking in a window at a wedding, and frightened people running all over and hiding.

God knows why.

(I don't mean God knows why they were hiding. I mean God knows why the picture was in a chip shop window).

I used to try to work it out, but I never did. It was a bit like these mysterious ads you see on TV where a football team chases a fat lady round a bus station until they are stopped by somebody on an elephant, and it's all supposed to make you want to buy some kind of soap powder.

The chips weren't as crispy at the bottom of Radford, but it had a sit-down section, two long well-scrubbed boards with benches, big battered metal salt-shakers and tubby vinegar bottles. You could eat your fish and chips right there and then on a plate, or order a "mixture" in a bowl. And you could even have a "mineral" with it - a *Vimto* or a *Tizer*.

A mixture was a sort of thick pea soup with chips in it eaten with a fork and spoon. You could also bring your own bowl or jug and take a hot mixture home. It looked pretty bad, but not as horrible as the livid green newspaper-wrapped pease-porridge I remember seeing somewhere else, probably in Breightmet, in Bolton.

But, to be fair, it was in Bolton that my mother took me to a very nice UCP. U.C.P. cafes (believe it or not, it stood for *United Cow Products*) were one of the North's nicest surprises. There was a posh one in Blackpool, somewhere near Hills' Bazaar where you had to queue for ages to get in, but it was worth it when you did. You sat down with your legs falling off after queuing for ages, in front of a snowy tablecloth with shining crockery and cruets, and your mother ordered plaice, chips and peas for everybody, a pot of tea and a plate of bread-and-butter and told you to sit up properly on your chair because people were looking at you.

Breightmet was where my Auntie Nellie and Uncle Jim lived then, and my two cousins, Charlie and Douglas, who could both kick a tennis ball in the air for hours on end, let alone a case-and-bladder football. There wasn't much chance of that with Uncle Jim hard-up on the dole and cycling all over South Lancashire with a hod on his shoulder looking for building sites.

Every now and then all Auntie Nellie's older sisters, Auntie Janet, and Auntie Lizzie from Radcliffe , my mother and Uncle Harold , the dancer, used to swoop down on Breightmet with a big parcel of fish and chips. and make a special tea.

On one of these visits, little Douglas looked up from a big plateful of chips over a pile of bread and butter and a bubbling glass of Dandelion and Burdock, and said "Ee, Mum, it's not so often we get a dinner like this is it?"

"Of course we do, Douglas. Eat your fish and chips, love." Auntie Nellie was embarrassed, but her sisters only laughed and rumpled the little lad's hair. That wasn't the biggest show-up in our family by any means.

My five-year-old Uncle David, who used to swear like a trooper, looked suspiciously at the cutlery and crockery my grandmother had borrowed from a neighbour for a special occasion. Then in front of the guests, he said bluntly "These aren't our cups and plates and knives and forks."

"Don't be silly, David," my grandmother told him, "Of course they're ours."

David gave the table one more searching look and then blurted out: " No they're not. _They're bloody Missis Mulder's!_ "

Douglas went on to play football for Bury, while I only went on to write all this nonsense about chip butties.

Untitled 4

When I was Only Five

When I was only five years old

And thought the world was made of gold

My mother took me to a farm

One summer day when it was warm

And there I spent the live-long day

Rolling and romping in the hay

Algy and Tusker (and Icky)

Uncle Harold was by far the most colourful person in our family. He was a bit light on his feet in more ways than one. My mother used to say that he had been spoiled by his four sisters, though it never dawned on me with my post-victorian upbringing that he was 'funny that way'. He was very handsome with wavy golden hair with a net over it. His sisters all treasured a profile photo of him in white evening dress. And he had *pals*.

He had served his time as a cotton-mill warper, before he went in full-time for dancing, and my mother treasured a cutting from the Bolton Evening News with a picture of him in a white tie and tails with the heading: "He's putting on his top hat". He had dance studios in unlikely places like the Orkneys and Belfast and even South Africa . He taught ballroom and tap dancing for Gem Waynefleet in London and Fred Astaire in New Mexico (of all "awful" places) , and toured in the chorus with Ivor Novello's *Dancing Years* . When it came to Manchester, his sisters brutally dragged their working-class heroes to watch him. The show ("We'll gather lilacs...") was hard for them to take, but not Uncle Harold, who was popular with everybody. I particularly remember going to a lunch he gave for us all at his flat in Crumpsall both because it was the first time I was ever in a "flat" , and the first time I ever got a bread roll next to my plate. Everybody laughed when I asked what it was, but I'll bet some of them (like my Dad, who had his "Spencer Tracy" suit on) didn't know either.

Once Uncle Harold worked as a steward on a cruise-ship and was seasick right round the world. We used to get postcards from Yokohama and that : "Sick again today!" . And at one time he was a sort of failed Jeeves, who finally did a daylight flit from a big country house, crouching behind the hedges. I have no idea why.

When he was called up in the R.A.F. one of his pals, Ray Thomas , who had long black brylcreemed hair , told us Harold knew more ways of dodging the column than anybody he ever met. Every now and then he would invite one of his sisters down to spend a glamorous week-end with him in London, where he had a flat in (pre-dosshouse) Leinster Gardens.

Apart from the pools, Dad and Mother had a small bet now and then (mostly *then*) on a horse, and one evening when they heard Owd Sammy Taypot shouting " Telly-graw! Last Pink! Telegraw!"up on Stansfield Street, I was given tuppence and told to go and buy a paper , running along the back street and up the steep stone steps to where Owd Sammy was standing under the yellow rays of the lamp post. I proffered my tuppence, and said politely, "A paper please, Mr.Teapot."

Owd Sammy, (whose real name – I learned afterwards- was Bickerstaff) exploded.

"Ah'll give thee Taypot, tha' cheeky little b*gger!" he shouted, hobbling towards me with a raised fist.

I shot down the steps, and dashed in through our back door as though Sammy was right on my heels, though in fact he was badly crippled , limping on the toe of one clog. When I dashed in through the back door , wild-eyed, my mother asked what was wrong with me, and I told her I'd just asked for a paper and the man tried to hit me.

"Well, what did you say?" Mother asked me, "were you cheeky?"

"No, I just said , "Could I have a paper please, Mister Teapot ?"

They couldn't stop laughing, but my mother finally told me why.

Then there was Mrs. Eccles (or just 'Eccles', usually). Eccles was a heavy old woman who used to sit out on her front steps across from the Top and tell me, sitting next to her, smelling a bit beery (her, not me) about *Icky*, this sort of creature she had down in her cellar. I used to ask her all kinds of questions about Icky, but as I still know nothing about him except that he lived in Mrs Eccles's cellar. She can't have told me much. I used to imagine him being big, and black as coal, and I supposed Eccles had to keep the cellar door shut to stop him coming out.

It went something like this:

"Tell me about Icky, Eccles."

"Aye, well, he's down in't coal cellar."

"Is he all black, Eccles?"

"Aye, all black, he is."

"Can I have a look at him, Eccles?"

"Oh no, that would never do."

"Why wouldn't it do, Eccles?"

I suppose any company is better than none, and she enjoyed pulling my leg, until (so my older sister Teresa tells me) I came home a bit unsteady and smelling of beer, and my mother had to go down and have it out with Eccles. I'd seen my mother get annoyed and I'd have backed her against Eccles any day. Icky as well.

There was also a strange little man who used to sit quite alone (as he thought) on a bench in Corporation Park. He would look round him to make quite sure nobody was watching, and then he would begin to rock backwards and forwards, slowly at first, and then faster and faster, singing over and over again to himself :

"Oh, Dorothy, Dorothy Day! ... Ohhhhh Dorothy Dorothy Dayyyyy....Ohhhhh Dorothy Dorothy Dorothy Dorothy Dayyyy...Ohhhhh!.. Dorothy..."and then he would stop suddenly and look furtively around as though there was somebody watching him critically from the bushes.

There was somebody watching all right, usually four of us; but we weren't watching critically. To us, in our early teens, he was just part of a very queer world in which nothing really made all that much sense. He was certainly no stranger than, say, the always-deserted "Conservatory", with a couple of rather doleful, much-initialled palm trees in the middle and some ferns, where Patch and I once walked up and down learning that noble poem *The Shooting of Dan McGrew* by heart while Nobby smoked a forbidden ciggy and Tony Connell just watched.

Even the Dorothy Day man was no stranger than the Catholic school we attended at the top of the hill, or the priests who taught us, John and his mint imperials, Poice and his big ginger fists, Billy Fish, Spud Murphy, Andy Cusack and his crimson lined cape and thick black leather strap, and above all big

Joe, who was as far beyond any mere human understanding as Mr. Micawber .

And come to think of it, he was no stranger than we were. There were a lot of religious ceremonies like "retreats" and lugging in the school meals boxes, but in winter we were unceremoniously pushed out into the cold and wandered about looking for shelter , up the road to Four Lane Ends where Blackburn suddenly fell towards Salmesbury or down past *The Hole In The Wall* pub to where the road plunged the other way down a cliff called Shear Brow. Just across from the school gates, Patch discovered a tiny Baptist Chapel, and when we went inside we found it was all jolly red velvet curtains and red velvet seats. There was even a notice on a board signed by somebody called Jolly, and "Jolly and his Iron Baptists" were duly entered, along with the entire school staff and various other grotesque characters, in the battered leatherbacked diary we simply called *The Play*.

Then there was Mr. Donnelly. Mr Donnelly was pointed out to me with awe by somebody when I was a kid. He had African spears on the walls at home and had been in Africa and all that.

Problem was, he was just *ordinary*.

I just couldn't believe that this little shirt-sleeved, flat-capped man with his limp and his Lancashire accent could possibly have been to Africa, where white men were either Tarzan or handsome moustaches in 'solar topees'.

Far more exotic was a strange old man called Mr. Howard used to turn up every summer at the house next door, separated from ours by a low wall and a small garden patch.

He wore a blazer and a straw hat which was fastened to his collar by a string, like someone too old auditioning for a part in *Salad Days*. What he had to do with the neighbours, I have no idea. He certainly didn't fit into a working-class district. However they were a rather funny family, with a boy who was sometimes called Abel Howard and sometimes called Abel Entwistle.

The mother was called *Ecksa*, which already struck me as a very improbable name but Jack Entwistle, who seemed to be her husband, was as common as they come, a short, thick man with a big boiled face, a cloth cap and a raincoat that looked dirty even in a town full of dirty raincoats.

Whenever he met me, he broke into a hoarse song:

"*Oh, Arthur,*

What've yer done to Martha?

Martha's not the same girl now..."

(Oh, Tee-hee.)

Anyway, every summer this mysterious old chap came to visit them for a couple of weeks and brought with him two dogs which never stopped barking. They were called *Algy* and *Tusker*, and they frightened the hell out of me.

They were terrier-size dogs, one was black with pointed ears and a curled-up tail, the other dirty white with black markings and brown ears.

I didn't know which was Algy and which was Tusker and it didn't matter. As soon as they saw me they came in a rush barking like mad. I suppose they enjoyed frightening me.

It did dawn on me, much later that they might probably be called *Elgar* and *Tosca*, but nobody at the time explained this to me, and it wouldn't have made a bit of difference if they had, as I'd never heard of either.

The only music I connected that family with was

"Oh, Arthur

What've you done to Martha..."

The real question though, was what Jack Entwistle had done to 'Ecksa'.

Feighting

For somebody who was never very good at fighting, I seemed to be in the thick of it a lot more often then I liked when I was a lad.

I wasn't as good at "getting the first one in" as some of my tougher schoolmates were from places like up Maitland Street and down Crown Street. In fact I must have been a sore trial to my Dad, who seems to have spent a lot of his bachelor days getting the first one in.

The line went a long way back on my mother's side too, at any rate as far as my Welsh coal-miner grandfather. He was once so sickened by the sight of Mr. Clay, the teacher, cutting up a sheep's eye, that he started retching. Mr. Clay cut at him with his cane, and my grandfather picked him up and stuffed him down the back of the hot water pipes. I suppose it was one way of leaving school.

I never saw anything like that at school, but I once saw a teacher - Owd Corran, I think it was - hotly pursuing Joe Harrison round the desks until Joe sensibly decided there was no future in it and made a bolt for the door. It was a hot summer day, the door was wide open, and I was sitting dreamily next to it. When the master shouted "Stop that boy!" it seemed to be me he was shouting to.

Big Joe thundered down the room at me with his iron-shod lace-up clogs going like sledgehammers. I made a ridiculous token pretence at grabbing his ragged jacket, and then he was gone, the din of his clog-irons gradually fading down the flights of stone steps.

On the other hand, I have seen some pretty violent set-to's between teachers and angry parents. I once saw a huge mother rush into a classroom wearing a "brat" - a sackcloth apron - all dripping with soapsuds, and wrap her meaty arms round a teacher. When she let go, he looked as though he had been in her tub and then through the squeezers.

Another time, the teacher was tipped off that the father of one of my classmates, a rag-and-bone man called Fitzsimmons, was coming to give him a thumping. He craftily waited for the ragman to climb sweatily up a long steep flight of stone steps, shouting abuse, and then *pushed* him.

With a great cry, the ragman toppled over backwards and rolled all the way to the bottom again. Luckily, he always wore two overcoats fastened round the middle with several turns of string - I remember him very well - and a large cloth cap, padded out, in the style of those far-off days - with newspaper. All the same, the fall took the steam out of him, and he limped off bruised and winded back to his donkey-cart, gay with goldfish bowls and coloured balloons full of bad breath.

In those days there weren't any of those little cardboard pumps to inflate balloons with. If you got a balloon from the rag-and-bone man (the going price was half-a-dozen jamjars) - he always blew it up for you first, and you carried it home like that. The chances were that sooner or later the kid who got the balloon would end up full of the ragman's breath as well. And there were of course the *Rubbing stones*, also given by the ragman in exchange for jamjars, that were used used to make a sort of yellow edge to your front steps.

"Give me a cream rubbing-stone if you've got one."

You never see rubbing stones these days.

I suppose there is a moral in this somewhere if I could just find it, but meanwhile I seem to be getting away from all the fighting.

Every now and then I got into a fight. I suppose there were lads who managed to steer clear of them, like my pal Allan, who was an altar-boy. Altar boys were sort of untouchables. But it wasn't easy for anybody else.

Perhaps the fact that my Mother never let me go to school with my shirt-tail sticking out through the back of my britches had something to do with it. I looked a bit soft.

There was a kind of ritual to it. The fights took place after school in a grim place at the base of an enormous smoke-stack, called "t'Mill Bottoms". The ground you fought and wrestled on was black dirt and cinders, useful for rubbing into your adversary's eyes. It happened to me, anyway.

In the school yard, the two fighters were surrounded by a swarm of bloodthirsty little devils shouting "A feight! A feight!" to attract other and swell the crowd. I hated it all. It used to frighten me, and it still does. But in spite of everything there was a kind of glamour about being the centre of a big crowd of boys, being pushed along to the place of execution, even when you were sure to end up with a nosebleed and a cut lip or worse. And then, there you were, struggling desperately in the dirt against somebody always stronger or more determined than you were. You were underneath with your nose pressed into the cinders and your mouth full of dirt, while somebody in ragged, evil-smelling britches sat on your head and thumped you in the ribs.

It isn't a thing I remember with any pleasure, but the sweat and blood and dirt seemed to be an unavoidable part of life then.

I should like to think we have got a little further today, but I have my doubts.

There was a small but energetic boy several years older than I was who lived further up the street. He sent me home with my nose bleeding a couple of times, and after all the rigmarole of getting me to lie on my back with a cold key down my neck and a wet cloth against my nostrils, my Dad decided that the time had come for boxing lessons.

It always seemed to work in library books and on the pictures ("Fetch Di Bando") when you trained and then beat the bully, usually bigger than you, too, not smaller, but I was never any good at it.

Dad, who was good at it, and had been an Army boxing semi-finalist, showed me how you didn't look the chap you were fighting in the eye, so he wouldn't know where you were going to hit him. I just didn't like hitting people enough.

Finally, after a couple of useless evenings with our shirts off (Dad, like a lot of other labourers in those days, had muscles like great eels slithering up and down his arms and I hadn't and haven't), he had a brainwave.

There *was* a boxer in the family. My cousin's husband, now a peaceful gardener, had boxed his way round fairgrounds and even reached the dizzy heights of a contest with Jake Kilrain.

I didn't know who *Jake Kilrain* was, but you had to respect anybody got into the ring to fight somebody with a name like that.

Besides, Ernie was interesting. He was a lean, sandy, mid-thirtyish man with a lot of time for youngsters and a large fund of stories about how he was attacked by a horde of rats in Norfolk, for example. Most of the stories came from the *Topical Times*, but he made them his own.

He had a bowler hat in the cupboard which he would pull down over his ears. He could make it bob up and down while he played an old piano-accordion. It made you laugh like anything. When I went to "train" with him on Wednesdays, he and my cousin Mary Ann would send me to the chip shop at the top of Carr Row for a "mixture", thick pea soup with golden chips floating in it.

In those days, the world heavyweight championships from America used to come through at about two in the morning, and sometimes I got to sit up with Dad to listen to Bob Bowman, who always sounded as though he was shouting in a storm, partly because of the transatlantic static, partly no doubt because of our *Osram Music Magnet*. Ernie, who had no wireless set, cycled through a real storm one morning to listen to the second Louis-Schmeling fight. He arrived, stripped off his wet raincoat, and went into the scullery to put the old iron kettle on.

"What I need is a right good cup of tea," he said.

"Louis leaped from his corner!" shouted Bob Bowman through the oscillations, "He caught Schmeling with a right! Schmeling's down! One, two, three...." and, as Ernie's head emerged from the scullery, jaw dropping in consternation and disgust,

"...nine, ten, OUT! It's all over!"

Now, admittedly, the piano-accordion and the chip suppers did very little to improve my boxing, but I did put in a few minutes on each visit shadow-boxing under Ernie's expert eye on the front parlour wall. I remember once or twice getting so excited that I bruised my fists on the wall, much to Ernie's glee.

Perhaps something did rub off after all, because my next bout with Terry, the smaller-but-older boy at the top end of the street was nearer a draw, after which, to my Dad's disgust and my Mother's relief, we called a truce and Terry took me to see their hen-pen and collect eggs.

The most successful fight I was ever in, I think, was one in which nobody struck a blow. As in most schools, the bigger boys at ours liked to experiment on the smaller ones in the interests of pure science. There were chiefly two kinds of experiment. One consisted of thumping a small boy to see what happened, and the other of egging two small boys on to thump one another. On this occasion I was one of the two small boys, and we had been coaxed and bullied into fighting one another though we were very friendly and flew paper aeroplanes together after school.

In those days, part of the normal clothing of boys was a very roomy cap with a large peak or "neb" as we called it, fastened up with a press-stud. It was very like the cap worn by all workmen, by my Dad, for instance. In fact it was social death for a working man to wear anything else. I have heard about one labourer who went to the factory in a "pork pie" hat and came back from the lavatory to find it had been nailed down to a bench.

As Derek and I joined battle, I grabbed the "neb" of his cap and pulled it down hard. The press-stud popped open, and the whole of Derek's face disappeared inside the cap. This tactic drew admiring comments from Jackie Gordon and the other lads who had egged us on, but they turned into jeers of disgust when I took to my heels and ran off up Spring Gardens while Derek was trying to get his cap off with one hand and punching out blindly with the other.

Jackie Gordon was particularly fond of punching smaller boys to see what would happen, which was always that they went home crying. I was one of them, and I suppose my mother had got fed up with it and decided to do something about it. On one never-to-be-forgotten afternoon, she came quietly down Spring Gardens while Jackie was demonstrating the hammer punch.

I had been chosen to assist in the demonstration, and had been pushed up against a broken board fence while Jackie hit me in the chest. He was enjoying himself so much that he didn't see what the gaping onlookers could see, my mother coming up behind him.

"And this," said Jackie with relish, clenching his fist, "is what we call "the hammer punch"!"

Mother swung an arm that had done a lot of hard work, and the slap caught Jackie over the ear. You could hear it all the way down Spring Gardens. He stood there for quite a while, lightning-struck, his mouth open, his eyes bulging, and his ear burning. Perhaps he was making a vow to give up hammer-punching small boys. At any rate, he left me alone after that.

There was a lot of cat-and-dog fighting between my mother and my Dad. It was worst when they did the wallpapering; you've put too much paste on, it's dripping on the floor; now you've cut the length too short; this roll doesn't match up; the swearwords flew thick and fast and it was best to get out from under the feet.

"Hold that edge up straight. No! Higher! No, Lower your end a bit!"

"Well, make up your *bloody* mind...!"

They used to fight over Dad's football pools, too. He always filled in the eight draws section (or whatever it was) by crossing off the eight last matches, which irritated my mother no end.

"They never come up like that!" she would tell him. "When did you ever see eight draws come up all together, one under the other? Why don't you spread them a bit? Cross one off, then leave a couple, then cross off another one or two. That's how they come up."

Dad always used the same crushing reply.

"They're not all playing on the same bloody field...!"

There was once a to-do about Dad stuffing out the front of his cap with pages from the Bible. He had an end drawer in the dresser with old bits of Bible in it, and Mother had somehow got it into her head that Dad used to tear pages out of the Bible to stuff the front of his cap with. *Why* he stuffed the front of his cap is another question altogether. I don't know. Perhaps it was some kind of fashion from *before* the Great War. Anyway, Mother got on to him.

It was asking for trouble, it would bring bad luck on us all, insulting the Bible like that. *Blaspheming*, that's what it was. Especially coming from somebody who in all the time she had known him, had never set foot inside a church. No wonder we never have any damned luck...

It went on for a long time before Dad got up in a rage, took his cap down from the back of the kitchen door and ripped a banana of yellowed newspaper out of it. It was from the *News of the World*.

But I think the fight I remember best from my childhood was the day when my Dad hit my mother. It happened on a Boxing Day, too.

What happened was this. Dad used to mend our shoes with bits of leather belting scrapped at the factory. He had an old black wooden box with a brass hook to keep it shut, and inside was his tackle; an old knife honed down to a razor-edge, an awl for pricking holes, some waxed strings he called "tatching-ends", his hammer, a cast-iron last with three legs, and some little triangular paper toffee-bags full of tiny brass nails. I used to be sent to ask for them in the Market Hall by the (to me) mysterious name of "five-eighths brass rivets".

He used to scrape a line about half-an-inch from the edge of the new soles he had cut out of the belting, and knock in these little nails all round the bottom of the shoe, where they shone in a pattern rather like that of the little silver cachous my mother used to decorate the tops of her trifles with.

As it happened, Mother had just made a trifle for us because it was Boxing Day. It stood on the table, three delicious layers of red sponge-jelly, yellow custard and a thick topping of cream in a big cut-glass bowl.

As Dad worked over a hundred hours a week, it was surprising to me that he was home at all, even on Boxing Day. But there he was, and for some reason- perhaps just sheer devilment - he decided to start mending shoes at about two in the afternoon.

He spread out his tackle on the hearth rug on an old *Advertiser*, got his cobbler's last between his legs, and started whittling away. After a few minutes the rug was covered with chips of leather. He seemed happy enough, whistling in a soft, breathy fashion old songs like "Comrades, comrades, ever since we were boys," and "Yip-aye-yaddy-aye-yay", but he must have been a bit out of temper, mending shoes just before dinner like that on Boxing Day.

Mother said nothing, though she didn't like it, but all at once she gave a cry of indignation and fished a bit of leather out of the trifle.

Then she really let him have it. What was the use of trying to give the children a proper Christmas when he was doing everything he could to spoil things for them. And just look at him! What other man sat about like that at Christmas? Why couldn't he try to smarten himself up. He looked like a bloody old tramp!

Dad sat there unshaved in his old union shirt with no collar, sleeves rolled up on his big forearms, his "weskit" frayed and shiny with wear and his pants covered with fragments of leather. He didn't say anything because his mouth was full of five-eighths brass rivets, but when Mother pushed past him angrily, he gave her a slap on the backside.

I don't suppose he hit her very hard but it certainly looked as though it hurt, but she was a Mitchell, (very distantly related to Scarlett O'Hara's Dad, I once heard) and she wasn't going to miss the chance of a starring role. She screamed and reeled back against the table. That did it, she told him - and us. That was the end.

"You've raised your hand to me for the last time!" she told him, "I'm leaving!"

Dad sat there with little brass rivets sticking out of his mouth, muttered "See if Ah keer," and pretended to root in his box.

We sat there worrying about whether Mother was going to leave home or not, and whether she would remember to put some trifle out for us before she went, and I suppose we cried as well while she got out a little cardboard suitcase with tin corners and began to pack some things in it. We had never seen Dad do anything like that before even when they were wallpapering, and we didn't know what to make of it.

I don't know what Mother packed, and I'm not sure she did. I was too busy crying as she went grimly up and down the stairs, slamming cupboards and drawers, and finally stood in the doorway in her old fawn coat and her U-boat hat (standing up in front like a German U-boat commander's) and delivered her parting shot:

"The meat will *burn* if you leave it in too long!"

Then she was gone.

We sat in front of the fire and cried like ventriloquist's dummies, wailing and swaying from side to side while Dad savagely stuffed his bits and pieces back into his box. Perhaps he was packing too? We wailed even louder.

"I think she's going to Radcliffe," Teresa told us, enjoying herself. That was where Mother came from, from distant parts on the other side of Bolton. "And she might not come back!"

She helped Dad, now in a much more sober mood, to get the dinner. He shaved with his cut-throat razor, the old one, because I had spoiled his new one by sharpening pencils with it. And he put on a clean shirt and even a collar and tie. If that didn't bring her home, nothing would.

We sat on a sort of bench Dad had made. (He made nearly all our furniture. You could tell.) We started playing our Friday night game . That was the night when Mother wen' shopping "down't street" and sometimes brought a couple of comics and a bag of toffees home with her. (I once asked her what the toffees she brought home were called and she told me they were "Lay'o'ers for meddlers". For years I thought that was the name of a special kind of toffee in crinkly paper).

On that Boxing Day, though, we played the Friday night game over and over until Dad must have been sick of it, though he didn't say so:

"She's just turned round the corner from the Main Road. She's walking up past the Nurse's Home. Now she's got to Holt's Meadow. She's reached the lamp. She's coming round the corner where Mrs Brown broke her leg.

"Past Mrs Chipchase's, Killalee's, Mrs Eccles's, Dunkinson's - past the back street. Now she's got to Kitty Rostron's. She's crossing the street! She's coming up our steps. one, two, three, four! She's on the top step! She's opening the door - <u>now</u>!"

But nothing happened. No Mother appeared, and we would go through it all again, time after time.

Finally, long after dark, when we were ready to give up, the door opened quietly, and there she was.

Dad stopped tinkering with the Osram Music Magnet and asked her if she could do with a cup of tea.

"I can get my own tea," she told him. Then she said, "If it hadn't been for these children, I wouldn't be here. Just so you know"

Dad didn't say anything, but the fight was over. I don't know who won. I did get some trifle, though.

'Vote, vote, vote, fer 'erbert Samuel.'

My Dad never went anywhere near a political meeting or made anything like a political statement that I can remember anyway. I think the nearest he came was right after Chamberlain's Sunday morning announcement that "a state of war now exists between England and Germany".

Dad said "That's it, then."

He did carry me down Johnny Wraith Broo on his shoulders one dark night in the thirties to watch the strikers coming up Bolton Road. To demonstrate outside *Fritz Hindle's*, if I haven't got it wrong. I'd heard they'd all be carrying torches, which sounded exciting, but they were only like little wooden pegs. My Dad wasn't in it. He had no time for either the bosses or the unions; he was the perfect democrat, equally incapable of giving and taking orders. He wouldn't join the union (they asked him to be secretary!). He said he didn't want the sweeper-up telling the boss what to do.

"So, Ah went up to see Young Jack (Watson). Thinks' world o' me, does Young Jack . "Hello, Hawwy (mincing voice), What's the trebble?" "Well, tha' knows me "- Ah tells 'im straight, Ah do, thinks *world* o' me..."

I used to listen to all this as a little lad, and even then, I never believed a bloody word of it. One slushy evening at the bottom of Belgrave Road as Dad and I turned the corner on the way home from the pictures. A posh car (<u>all</u> cars were posh then) drove past, splattering us hoi-polloi without slowing down and whizzing off down Market Street.

"That's that bloody silly Jack Watson!" Dad fumed, "I'll give it the bugger tomorrer!"

But I know he didn't..

My Mother was different, she was what used to be called "a red-hot Liberal" which now sounds a bit of a contradiction She used to take me with her to political meetings where they all sang "Vote, Vote, Vote fer 'Erbert Samuel ", and his daughter Nancy, who at any rate didn't turn her back on the Liberals and run for Labour like Lord George's daughter Megan did.

In the middle of the war, Honour Balfour who was a journalist with *Picture Post* stood in a by-election when you weren't supposed to, and my Mother took me to all her meetings . I remember her looking plump and clean, with a little scarf round her neck, and she sounded sensible to me because everybody cheered. She got beaten by Stuart Russell who went on winning for the Tories for *ages*. Why he kept getting in I don't know, it seemed a bit queer in a completely working-class town with just a few doctors and solicitors. But it seemed to me that the Liberal candidates weren't up to much, and I remember once at a small meeting actually asking one of them a question about free trade and then arguing with him. I didn't know anything about free trade and I still don't, but it turned out that he didn't either. My mother never got over it, she was so proud that her son had a turn for politics, actually standing up and asking a question, why Harry would never have done that in a thousand years.

I went to hear Harold Macmillan supporting the Tory member at the Baths, and sat on the back row, where

Mac stood waiting for a moment before walking down the hall to be introduced by the chairman.

Suddenly, the old chap next to me looked up, saw no less than *Harold Macmillan in the flesh* standing right next to him and screamed with surprise. *He* gave me a real shock, but Mac , who (I read somewhere) had a couple of medals for bravery , never so much as looked down.

Anyway, I was careful who I sat next to when I went to hear Captain Attlee, as the old brigade called him. But the best of all the Labour speakers was tiny George Tomlinson. Most people thought of him as a second-rater, but at the Weaver's Institute on the Green , he had a crowd of workers eating out of his hand. He blamed his small, rather humped, body on Tory malnutrition. "When I first got to Westminster", he told us, "I used to wonder why all the chaps on our side were all five foot six, and all the chaps on the Tory benches were six foot five. And one day I put it to the Missus, I said "I wonder why it is, that all the chaps on our side are all five foot six, an'all the chaps on the Tory benches are all six foot five." "Never you mind, George, " she said, "They measure 'em *from the neck up* here, luv."

And he finished with a story about Ernest Bevin at an infant school , walking hand in hand with a little child :"and if we all just put our hands in the hands of the little children….." It had us all standing up and cheering. It was a pity I was too young to vote, though I was soon old enough to have my first passport with a declaration beginning : "*We*, Ernest Bevin…"

Randolph Churchill drew a lot of people to the Coop meeting hall just after the war and turned them against his Dad and the sunny Tory uplands with a speech which nobody ever forgot , telling us, standing there in our caps and mufflers, that if Labour got in, they'd tax everything, including " *your* beer, and *my* whisky…".

"Aye," somebody shouted, "and thi Dad's bloody big fat cigars!"

Sir William Beveridge was a lot more brilliant, but he didn't do much better at the Coop meeting hall , explaining his famous Report for the Welfare State. He had a lot of white hair and a lean eager face, and blinded us all with science. At question time, a small, rather stout man at the front stood up and said in a loud, carrying voice:

"I represent the *'oddlesden Pig-Keeper's Association, also* the *'oddelsden Poultry-Keeper's Association*, and I would like to ask Sir William Beveridge what he plans to do for *us*."

Beveridge smoothed back his long white hair and said something like, "Section Seven , Paragraph Nine will take care of that. Next question?"

The small, rather stout man took a step forward and shouted: "I represent the 'oddlesden Pig-Keeper's Association, also the 'oddelsden Poultry Keeper's Association, and I want to know what you are going to do for us!"

Beveridge began to recite Section Seven, Paragraph Nine from memory, but I don't think anybody understood any of it, certainly not the representative of the two 'o.P.P.'s who finally had to be hushed down by the crowd.

The Boy With a Book

My Dad was very impressed by my cousin Charlie's knowledge of football. Charlie, who was a bit older than I was, and his younger brother Douglas, who played for Bury later on, were football dotty and could run rings round me dribbling a tennis ball over the cobblestones in the back street . I remember Dad once withering me with a report of what Charlie could do with the *Bolton Evening News*.

"He just runs his eye down't results, and Jim'll say, like, "'Ow did Wanderers get on, Charlie?" "Won, Dad, two-nowt!" Or, he'll ask him, "What about City?" "Drew wi' Burnley, Dad, two apiece!"

Then running a resigned eye over me and my Wizard, he would add with a sniff,

"And....thee..."

"Leave him alone, Harry!" Mother would say, "He does his best. I expect he knows more about some things than Charlie does."

"Aye. Happen he does. What things? He allus has his head buried in a bloody comic..."

I think the first weekly comics we took were *Chips* and *Funny Wonder*.

I read somewhere that the comic strip about *Weary Willie and Tired Tim*, the two tramps in Chips, was the world's first, and whilst I can't vouch for that, I remember the two tramps all right, one short and fat and dark, the other long and bony and looking a bit like Uncle Sam, though I couldn't say offhand now which was Weary Willie and which was Tired Tim, but I remember one saying how wonderful it would be if you could just get anything you needed by pushing a button, and the other saying " Oh, yeah, who's going to push that button?" It wasn't my first joke, my Mother's joke came first.(Remind me to tell it to you.) But nearly.

The drawings were just black-ink but the paper was a sort of pinkish colour. I suppose the idea was to get a bit of colour in *somehow*. After all, when TV was just black-and-white, some people bought a sort of filter to fit over the screen, half green and half blue. The Duttons had one, next to us in Belgrave Road. Outside scenes with sky and fields looked nice. But most TV scenes show streets or rooms or just talking heads, and people with blue heads and green trousers looked a bit odd.

I can dimly remember *Tiny Tots* and *Chicks' Ow*n though I have a feeling that these weren't the children's comics we took first. Ragged copies of *Tiger Tim's Weekly* came our way occasionally.

But a little later, *Jingles* and *Tip Top* lay behind the front door every Tuesday and Wednesday. Tip Top was all green, and Jingles usually all white - with flour perhaps, because my Mother baked on Tuesdays, laying out rounds of dough to rise on floury sheets of newspaper. I used to read the comic, keeping one eye on the baking, while she spread muffins and sadcakes on the tabletop laid with flour-covered newspapers. Sadcakes, full of currants, stayed flat after they had been baked, but the muffins swelled up into big juicy wheels. Mother cut them into thick boats and we ate them hot from the oven, spread with melting butter and strawberry jam.

With the smell of the muffins filling the house, I used to spread my comic on the floury table and spell through a serial story about an English boy in a desert. There was a picture of him with an Arab headdress on outside a tent.

It was these comics that got me reading. When I was six, Miss Finn took me across the yard to the big boys' school to read for the headmaster, Mr Toole, a heavy man with a grey moustache who tried me with *Hiawatha*, but it was too hard. Still, he went and fetched a big rusty biscuit tin and took out a little bag of boiled sweets for me as a reward for not being able to read Hiawatha.

When I was seven I had got as far as the D.C.Thompson comics, and like every boy of my age, I learned to read by reading the *Adventure,* the *Skipper,* the *Rover,* the *Hotspur* and the *Wizard,* with the *Champion* and *Triumph* running them close and the *Magnet* dragging its heels behind.

My Mother told me that my Uncle Arthur, who worked in an enormous cotton mill with blazing windows, used to read old Billy Bunter boarding school comics, the *Gem* and the *Magnet* with all that 'Yaroo, leggo you beasts, Ha! Ha! Ha!' stuff, tuck boxes and dorm feeds, the *Shell* and the *Remove* (whatever they were). But I didn't much care for the public schools stories. Of course there was *Mustard Smith* in the Adventure, a boarding school master who was called that because he was as keen as mustard on football and cricket. And *Red Circle School* in the Hotspur was a bit more to my taste than Billy Bunter's "Greyfriars".

But what about the headmaster who used to sniff maddening fumes at night from a brazier in his room, and then run round the countryside with nothing on, worrying sheep? (Worrying sheep by the way didn't mean that he was just sort of bothering them. He was tearing their throats out with his teeth!) Would you want to go there? I couldn't see Mr. Toole doing it.

The Adventure and the rest taught us all to read. The first time I opened an Alistair Maclean thriller, I could see that he had had the same teacher as I had, though he must have done his homework better.

You had to be able to read properly then because there weren't any pictures with speech balloons except in the Yankee Comics you bought now and then from Mr Forrest in the Market Hall. A story in the Adventure or the Wizard would have one amazing picture, and the rest was all print. One of my favourite pictures was the heading to a story called *The March of Ten Thousand Gorillas*. It showed you a gorilla army, winding back over hill and valley, all marching in step about six abreast, each one with a big club smartly carried over the left shoulder. Where they were marching to, I couldn't say now, but I certainly tried to find out then. I have a feeling they were out for revenge on some poor devil or other. There was a plague of giant rats, too, that rather worried me, at the time, but I'm not going to plague you with it, or with a list of all the stories we read.

Still, I have to mention *Grob* in *Ten Thousand Years Ago*, who invented things like fire and the wheel, while all my Dad ever invented or at any rate "fettled", was an alarm clock that would only go on its side in the oven. And *Ten Terrible Tasks for Trapper Tim*, who went round loaded down with an amazing assortment of gear including ropes and a ladder and a mongoose in a basket on his back because they might come in useful. And there was *Chang the Hatchet Man*, and the *Wolf of Kabul* with twin daggers, and his pal *Chung*, with his bloodstained cricket-bat bound with copper wire, *Blue Dragon Pyke, Lionheart Logan, Strang the Terrible* with his stone club, *The Black Sapper, Trig M'Fee* and *Black Norton*, and ...oh, all the dozens of others I remember but am not going to bother you with.

Solo Solomon was rather special though, a cowboy who talked to his horse *Gasbag* and got funny answers from it because he was a ventrilo...well, he could, like, throw his voice. There were fascinating ads, too.

When I saw an ad in one of the comics offering to teach me how to throw my voice for a couple of bob, I pestered my Dad for the money, and waited excitedly for the great secret to arrive. It turned out to be a little booklet telling you to try talking without moving your lips, practicing phrases like "a gottle of geer" and "grown gread and gutter". There was one of those little leather bird warblers in it as well. It stuck to the roof of your mouth and you could produce a high-pitched, irritating squeak with it. After a day or two mine disappeared, though whether it was because my Mother was scared of me getting it stuck in my windpipe or (as I suspect) just couldn't take the squeaking any more, I couldn't say.

I can't say, either, that I practiced "a gottle of geer" much either, so I never became a ventrilo... a Solo Solomon.

Comics cost tuppence apiece. I used to swap the Wizard every week for Frank McHugh's Adventure. That still wasn't enough reading, but I usually managed to beg another tuppence off my Dad on Friday nights when he came home to tip his wage up and get his ten-bob spending money, before he went off to the Brit for a couple of pints and came home jolly and reddish-faced and spent up.

Then I would set off along the darkened street on the way to Mr. Kay's, the newsagent's on the Main Road. I didn't need to cross the road, but I had to go down Spring Gardens and past the Bottoms, a dark clump of trees and bushes behind a disused cotton mill. I had heard that there were rats down there, and my head was full of giant rats and even giant gorillas. Still, I have to have a comic, so I used to run fearfully down the steep pitch-dark lane, scampering past the Bottoms with my tuppence clutched firmly in a grubby fist. Coming back was even worse, and as a kind of flimsy protection against hurtling rats (I had heard they always went for your throat) I used to stuff my copy of the Rover down the front of my jersey so that it stuck up underneath my chin, and sprint desperately uphill in the dark. Once I got back home, lying on the rug in front of the fire with my comic open at The Black Sapper, my natural bravery always came back with a rush.

Milner Hatpin (as he was known) used to come round with a huge bunch of tattered comics to swop. My mother wasn't very keen on Milner's comics because they were probably full of germs from the dozens of hands they had been through, but we swopped with him anyway, we didn't care about the germs. Another way of getting comics was from Mr Forrest's, a small bespectacled man who made a living in the Market Hall by exchanging comics. The strange thing about his stall was that while he wouldn't take anything but clean, new-looking copies dated a week or two back at the most, his stall was piled high with tattered, scrofulous-looking comics which must have come from somewhere. You could change a new Wizard for an ancient torn one on a one-to-one basis.

But Mr Forrest also had Yankee comics, little comic books from across the Atlantic long before World War Two. They had not been sold separately as comic series are now. They had originally been give-away supplements to American newspapers, with a lot of variety in them, a few exciting pages of heroes like *Tarzan, Flash Gordon, Buddy Rogers, Dick Tracy* (*Superman* had not yet arrived) funnies like, *Joe Palooka, Li'l Abner, Etta Kett, Fritzi Ritz, Nancy, Blondie, Bringing up Father, The Little King, Henry, Smokey Stover, Snuffy Smith, Harold Teen,* many of them with speech balloons and all of them in colour. The fact that I can roll the names off after so long shows what an impression they made on me. And on my sisters, too, who used to read Yankee comics (though there was more to look at in them than to *read*). Being girls, though, they weren't too interested in stuff like The Wolf of Kabul, Chung's "yellow, broken teeth" and his bloodstained "Clicky-Ba".

We took the Girl's Crystal for a while, which I read of course because I read everything I could get hold of, even the *Empire News* and *John Bull*, but the stories always seemed to be about whether this desperate-looking girl in a gymslip would be dropped from the hockey team because she had been falsely accused of lying; or whether Sally and Fay were misjudging Johnny. There wasn't a gorilla in sight, never mind ten thousand of them, just as there weren't any girls in any of the D.C. Thompson boy's papers. I'd certainly have missed the gorillas more in those days, though girls got more important for us Wizard-readers later on.

My mother read a lot of books but they mostly came from the twopenny lending library in the Market Hall, and were written by chaps called Netta Muskett, Ethel M. Dell, and Ruby M. Ayres. They were usually about an ugly but secretly rich chap whose face was "transformed" every now and then by a beautiful smile he could turn on when he was solving some girl's problems for her. He always turned out to be well off and they got married at the end.

I liked the beautiful smile idea, and tried an experimental smile or two myself in a rather flyblown mirror we had upstairs. I couldn't get it quite the way I wanted it though, it was more like a snarl. Perhaps that's why I never solved any girl's problems for her. To be quite honest, I'm afraid I've actually created problems for one or two.

My Mother also read a weekly women's magazine printed on a kind of coarse black-and-white paper called *The Miracle* because it was a miracle that anybody ever bought it.

The main story was called *Martha Strang - Murderess*, and it went on for months. They never caught her, at any rate not until after Mother stopped taking it, and I don't suppose they ever will, now.

Mother read *Dracula* before I was born, running up the dazzlers after Dad at bedtime, shouting for him to wait. As a matter of fact I once thought my Dad was a vampire. I woke up one morning and found myself in bed with a total stranger; he had gone to bed with his teeth in and they must have slipped out a bit while he was asleep. I slipped out as well and got in with my Mother.

I moved on to another level of reading when I bought an old copy of *Westward Ho!* at a jumble sale in St. Joseph's infant school. I bought it along with a little lead anchor for twopence, and I must have got pretty near the middle when I found out that there were forty pages missing, so it got thrown out into the coal hole just westward of the back door to the scullery. Dad had put up a swing in the door frame and you could swing back into the kitchen and then forward into the coal-hole, over the coal. I didn't find out what happened to Amyas Leigh and the beautiful native princess Ayacanora until years later, and now I've forgotten, but I expect she ended up running a boarding-house in Torquay.

Soon after that I joined what Owd Tommy Oldham at the end of the street, a small, tough eighty-year-old who never wore an overcoat or a raincoat in his life, used to call the Bloodsucker's Library, his name for the *Andrew Carnegie Free Library* at the top of School Street, which ran up from the Blackburn-Bolton Road. It was a fine building, with an imposing drawbridge entrance over a kind of deep dry moatinto a wide foyer for newspapers, a children's library, and (the holy of holies) the adult lending library along with with a big reading room where you sat down and took off your cap to read the *Sketch*, the *Sphere* and the *Tatler* with photos of upper class people ("Mrs Rees Foxton-Withers, relaxing on her shooting- stick, shares a joke with Colonel Ponsonby") and a reference library where almost nobody ever went and there was a big folio copy of *The Ancient Mariner* with pictures.

At first I only had a ticket for the children's section, but Uncle Jim Rostron who was out of work like nearly everybody else, with a mouth full of bad teeth because he couldn't afford to have them pulled out, let alone get false ones, got me useful educational works like Cherry Kearton's *Photographing Wild Life Across the World* and Frederick Mars's *Heart of the Ancient Wood* until I was old enough to read A.G. Hales's *McGluskies* and Maurice Walsh (see below!). Uncle Jim had a copy of *Livingstone's Travels* on a table in his little front parlour open at a picture of a crocodile with a black girl in its jaws, and underneath, it said *In the Grip of the Monster*. I can still call up that picture when I want to, and sometimes when I don't.

I liked animal books. I read and reread one story – I forget which book it was in – called "Rusty Roustabout" about a little wirehaired fox terrier marooned on an island in the backwoods that chased a big lynx until it caught him. It was just about to rip the little terrier open when this chap shot it.

The father of one of the young men my older sister Teresa was always getting engaged to, once asked me what I wanted to be when I left school and I told him I wanted to be a gamekeeper so I could watch all these fantastic goings-on in the woods. He smoked his pipe for a bit over that one, and then told me I should try to get on as an electrician or a plumber because that was where the good money was.

I had wondered now and then where the good money was (*my* family certainly didn't know) and the only thing I knew about electricity, from having to help Dad to mend the Osram Music Magnet ("Just get howd of that wire a minute" "Oh, no, Dad, please! Owww!!) wasn't encouraging and I never got into it (or the money either), though my best pal Alan did. When he got into his teens his Dad wouldn't let him go out after work. He had to study for his City and Guilds, whatever they were, so we only followed girls at weekends. I mean, I couldn't very well have followed them on my own, could I?

A bit later on, I got my own ticket to the adult library. There were no seats in the lending library which was tough on a boy's legs, standing there for hours propping up a book against the shelves, I read practically anything, mainly serious educational stuff like A.G. Hales's McGlusky books ; Maurice Walsh's small dark Irishmen biffing big blond Anglo-Saxon brutes; Edgar Rice Burroughs (*Tarzan* teaching himself to read ,and *John Carter Warlord of Mars*); Rafael Sabatini's *Cap'n Blood,*; Ernest Thompson Seton (" Lobo, King Wolf of Corrumpaw") ; Olaf Stapledon's *Odd John* (his first words in the pram were "I've finished mathematics") ; Zane Grey ("Hell-bent Wade"); Anthony Hope's *Zenda* novels; and so, over the years, on to Wells, Kipling, Chesterton, Hemingway, Huxley and the non-fiction shelves, where I used to put a tram-ticket in a book to find my place next day. There wasn't all that much activity there in contrast to the *Books Returned* section ,buzzing with people finding out whether a book was a good read from the number of date stamps at the front.

My father never went to the library himself, but every now and then he used to ask me to get him "the best book he had ever read", a Western called "The

Lightning Bug". I never found it, and as I matter of fact I still haven't. I did experimentally get him *Jane Eyre* once. Only once. Luckily, the back door was open.

Kesmus

On Christmas Eve my Auntie Lily and Uncle Johnny came from Hacking Street with my cousin George who was a grown-up to me, and Emily and Jack. Jack was George's married older brother and Emily reminded me of Irene Dunne. She giggled and had a crush on Gary Cooper.

There was always a green tin of chocolate biscuits, fingers, wafers, ovals, and George always ate nearly all of them. I know that because Mother could start telling me about it any time in the year, on the early workman's bus to Bolton, for example, it annoyed her that much.

And there was Port Style Ruby Wine, and a bottle or two of ale and beer with names like Big Ben and O.B.J. (I think it stood for "Oh, Be Joyful", and they all were, except possibly Mother watching George having another chocolate biscuit, and bustling in and out of the kitchen.)

I can't remember now if there was a sit-down meal or not, but probably we had meat sandwiches. Mother knew how to cook a juicy joint and cut big moist slices, so what with the beer and the crisps, and *Wills' Whiffs*, and the home-made fruit cake in a sort of hula-hula skirt, and what was left of the chocolate biscuits, our visitors from Hacking Street must have looked forward to their Christmas Eve as much as I did.

Of course, Christmas Eve wasn't a patch on Christmas Day, but it showed we were getting there at last. I seem to remember myself always sitting on the floor, watching, at the side of the tall sewing machine. We called it "the sewing machine", though I can't recall ever having seen any machine on it. It was flat on top and polished, underneath a little lace tablecloth, and later, when we had a wireless, the speaker stood on it. But at floor level, where I lived, there was a little iron tread-plate you could move up and down. That sewing-machine had a kind of old-fashioned style to it, and you couldn't knock it over, either. Hitler tried.

I didn't take much part in the proceedings, though I was once allowed to try Uncle Johnny's whiff and it caused a lot of coughing and laughing. Pleasures tended to be simpler in those days.

Bedtime and Come on, let's have you up them dancers. Climbing the stairs to the chilly back bedroom with the big Osram battery-lamp throwing ghosts round the varnished banisters, across the big flock bed and up the wallpaper. The battered brass bedknobs gleaming, shadows scampering across the ceiling and Uncle Johnny laughing at something downstairs.

And then the long wait of anything up to six months, not for Father Christmas to come, but for Father Christmas to have *been*, with your feet toasting on the flat, News-Chronicle-wrapped oven plate.

I suppose we dropped off at last, my small sister and I, though looking back you seem to have been awake all night. My older sister Teresa (only everybody had to call her Terry in those days) was in the know, and she used to get up "to make a cup of tea for Father Christmas", which sounded reasonable, though if he had a cup of tea in every house, he must have had the classic visiting-curate's problem pretty badly.

At this point we would bounce about the bed shouting "Has he been yet?" and Teresa would keep bring us reliable downstairs news like "I'm just helping him to decorate the Christmas tree" or "I'm just making him a sandwich before he goes."

At last, the great moment arrived. My father would stand at the bottom of the stairs and blow a little glass trumpet from the Christmas tree. (It was many years later, tuning a guitar, that I realised the trumpet's note was a perfect A.)

We tumbled down the dark stairway and there at last, was Christmas. We stood blinking and wondering at what we saw, Mother and Dad watching *us* and, as I know now, feeling much the same way we did.

The beautiful tree stood on the table, with all its little wax candles alight, covered with chocolate ornaments, little gold nets of chocolate coins, rabbits and gnomes and Father Christmasses galore, all in coloured silver paper. There were glass globes, one with a spire on it at the top of the tree, reflecting candlelight and firelight.

In pyjamas we buried ourselves in the pillowcases laid out beside the table, pulling out present after present. I can't remember ever being disappointed. You never told Father Christmas what you wanted in those days. He already knew.

Every year, I got a *Billy and Bunny* annual: and over the years there would be other books of boy's stories, lead soldiers in a long box with little flattened canvas tents you could put up, a bakelite house-building set, a car kit you could fit different bodies on, a space gun that used big rolls of paper instead of caps. and made an ear-deafening noise, games like ludo, draughts or snakes and ladders, a chocolate "smoker's outfit", a chocolate "selection box", a big tin of caramels, perhaps a wind-up train set, a cowboy outfit...

There was hardly time for me to admire the gifts, dolls, a dolly's pram, doll's clothes, held up by my small sister with little screams of pleasure. But she had plenty of other admirers.

One of the more sensational presents I got was a man-sized bow and arrow set. The bow was bigger than I was, and the arrows were tipped with brass cones. I was very excited about it, but as I couldn't manage it too well, and I couldn't play with it in the street, Dad took me up on the moors to the Blue Delph to try it out, and he tried it first. When the arrow whizzed across the slopes and buried itself up to the end feathers in a pile of shale, I was a lot more delighted about it than he was. I expect he was imagining what would happen if I had a practice shot at somebody's chest.

I never knew who bought me the bow and arrow set, and I never found out what happened to it. It was one of the inscrutable problems of childhood.

The bunny in my *Billy and Bunny Book* wasn't our only traditional Christmas rabbit. My mother always made a rabbit pie for Christmas Day.

I can remember her teasing us in the kitchen, showing us the skinned carcass, asking if we didn't feel sorry for the poor little rabbit. But a skinned rabbit doesn't look like much to a child. She had more success with the little plasticine sheep she used to make, and the plasticine wolf that came to gobble them up. That generally got the childish screams of protest she enjoyed.

Cooked in a big brown pot with stewing steak, and a crisp brown crust on top, and flanked with floury potatoes and other vegetables, the rabbit made a delicious Christmas dinner. But sitting down to enjoy it was a another thing altogether, because there always seemed to be somebody ill that day. I remember the ambulance waiting, and Mother bustling into her coat while my small sister Margaret was taken to hospital with scarlet fever. I think it was when my big sister Teresa was being carried downstairs with diphtheria that I made my notorious appeal to Mother, handed down through the years:

"Can't you just put some rabbit pie out for me before you go?"

It was a big thing when one of my sisters was up at Bull Hill. I never got there, (I don't think visitors were allowed in anyway) so to me it was just some gates you went passed on the way to Bolton. Once when I bicycled past, there was a huge tub outside the gates, filled high with bloodstained bandages.

Every few days I had to go Down't Street to the Market Hall, and look at a little glass case outside the "health office", where there was a list of numbers that were "progressing favourably".

We once went to Auntie Lily's for Christmas dinner. All along the lobby and all round the walls of the parlour, where there was a fire burning for Christmas, there were black and white photographs of Uncle Johnny, who drove the corporation muck cart, holding the heads of enormous glossy horses decorated with big brass ornaments. Uncle Johnny had won a lot of prizes, mostly big coloured ribbons and cards, with his horses. If you looked closely, you could recognise George or even Jack on some of the pictures, sitting on the backs of the horses.

I have a faint recollection that we once had a goose for dinner at Auntie Lily's At any rate, I can remember Uncle Johnny telling us proudly that he could "pick a boo-un as clean as onny dug" . When he said it, I was sitting in the middle of the staircase, looking at them all, round the table, through the banisters, (it was a funny shape, that house) and I saw Bob's little black-and-tan terrier face, down on the hearthrug, get even longer and thinner.

On the sink there was a little dead pigeon on its back with a bead of blood at the corner of its beak. When I asked George why it had died, he told me it was for a pigeon pie, but I of course knew he was just being silly. Perhaps they were going to have it stuffed, like the birds under a glass dome in Uncle Jim Rostron's front room.

We once had a goose. My Dad won it in a Christmas raffle at work, and my mother was all smiles and laughing expectation until he brought it home under his arm, hissing. When he put it down in the kitchen it went for everybody in sight, with that long neck stretched out and those great big wings beating.

"It's just like you, you big silly fool," she told him,

"Whatever are we going to do with that thing? Get back, go on, get back!" She had to keep it off with the long brush.

I think they patched up an uneasy truce after a while, at any rate I remember Mother feeding it bits of bread in the back yard. And then they sold it to somebody because she couldn't fancy eating something she had fed.

Now turkey was another matter. We had tasted turkey because Mrs Smith at the off-license next door used to give my mother the rather strong-smelling remains of their Christmas turkey (nobody had a fridge in those days). Helping Mother to pick the bones, avoiding the sage-and-onion as best I could, left me with a kind of sneaking sympathy for vultures.

One of my most vivid Christmas memories is one of lying on the carpet at the side of the table with the Christmas tree on it. I was eating caramels out of one of those big round tins children got in the days before anybody bothered about teeth. I was reading a story in a Christmas annual, with a black and white picture of somebody in a boat shooting at a crocodile. There was a roasting coal fire, and my mother was bustling about as usual getting the dinner ready. And suddenly I found myself wondering whether I was enjoying myself. Was this what-you know - what real happiness was like, what really enjoying yourself was like, lying there with a mouthful of sweet, sticky caramel, reading about adventures in the jungle, and your bare legs getting mottled with the heat of the fire.

Just for a moment, it seemed to me that, somehow, I wasn't *inside* the toffee-chewing any more than I was inside the adventure - or the toffee tin for that matter. And it seemed to me, funny suspicious kid that I was, that it couldn't be the proper thing, not real enjoyment, because you couldn't watch yourself having real enjoyment and wondering if it *was* real. When you really *were* enjoying yourself, surely you couldn't think about it like that?

I suppose that was as close as I have ever got to what they call an out-of-the-body experience, and while it wasn't all that close, it's funny that I've remembered it all these years. So I think there's a certain amount of truth in it, at any rate for me. The only enjoyment you can *both* feel <u>and</u> watch, I think, is when you are giving pleasure to somebody else, or even just watching them being happy. That's the kind of pleasure my mother and dad got out of Christmas, along with a glass or two of ruby style port and a rabbit pie in a big brown pot with a brown crust on it.

So most of Christmas was just enjoying myself without knowing, then, that I was doing it, and enjoying other people being happy in their different ways.

Children in Europe don't know what it's like to lie awake all night waiting for Father Christmas to have been, because they get their presents on Christmas Eve. I don't know whether that's better or not. It's a kind of torture, wishing the time would go quicker, but once you've got your presents, no matter how much you like what you get, the most exciting part is over. My younger sister and I probably got some sleep, but all you remember is the waiting, and shouting downstairs,

"Has Father Christmas been yet?"

We could hear suggestive noises downstairs. We knew that our older sister was allowed to go downstairs before we were, "to make Father Christmas a cup of tea", but we had to wait until somebody -Dad, I suppose - blew a little glass trumpet at the bottom of the stairs to let us know we could come down.

There was always a big fire, as we were in pyjamas, but we weren't sharp enough to wonder how Father Christmas got down the chimney without being burnt. The Christmas tree stood there, covered with chocolate ornaments, with all its candles shining. Coming out of the darkness, you had to screw up your eyes to look at it.

The tree, all of four feet high, lived in the bottom drawer of the cupboard, wrapped up in newspaper. You folded it up like an umbrella. It wasn't made of plastic, because nothing was in those days. But its branches were covered with dark green needles, and when they were opened out, and hung with chocolates and glass ornaments and tinsel and coloured candles, it looked wonderful. To us, anyway. I have had Christmas since with people who have to have a real fir tree ten feet high, with handmade ornaments and snow-white candles. And with people who have to have a tree that changes colour in time to Christmas music. But, to us, a Christmas tree was something you got out of the bottom drawer and opened like an umbrella. There is still a little boy inside me that tells me that all fir trees ought to be able to fold up in the same way, no matter how big they are, even the double-crowned one outside in my garden, which must be about forty feet high.

Wasting a Cephos

There was something called *Penny Headache Powders* which did my Mother's head a world of good (we gave her a lot of headaches), but they were not easy to get hold of, and I was usually sent across the low wall (we lived next to Smith's off-licence) for two *Cephos* powders. They cost two pence each. I didn't know why they were called Cephos, but they were powders.

It was all right as long as my mother or my Dad took them and not me. Mother would get herself half-a-glass of water, carefully unfold the queer paper full of white, flour-like powder, crease the paper down the centre and channel the powder on to her tongue. Then she would make a wry, bitter face, and take a drink of water. And if she got the chance, she would have five minutes in the rocking-chair, shutting her eyes and wondering whether any little fairies would tidy up a bit while she had a nap.

The trouble was that every now and then you had to have a Cephos powder yourself, and that raised problems, because not only did the stuff taste horrible, but it had to be got down somehow.

Mother would fold up the paper and try to pour it on to your tongue, but it got up your nose and into your lungs, and if you coughed or sneezed, the Cephos powder went all over the place.

"Ooh! He's wasted a See-fuss! He's wasted a Seefuss!" Margaret would shout.

"Ee! You silly little bugger!" Mother would tell me, "Look what you've done. All over me and all over the floor. They cost two pence apiece, Cephoses...!"

Then you might get another one in a spoon mixed with milk, and you had to get it down while the inside of your nose was stinging with bitter powder.

Cephos powders were what you usually had in those days if you were ill, but there was a whole range of other things to get you better. You only went to the doctor if you were on your last legs, "bringing up lumps of phlegm as big as a pint-pot" as one old lady put it. I do wish I hadn't heard her, because the phrase has haunted me for about fifty years, and now it's all yours...

We bought quite a lot of lung-healers. I used to be sent to Smith's for a pennyworth of lung-healers and come back with them at the bottom of a a little triangular toffee-bag. If you didn't actually know there were lung-healers in it, you would have thought the bag was empty, because a lung-healer was about the size of a full-stop.

How anything that size could possibly heal your lungs remains a mystery to me. It wasn't easy to swallow a lung-healer, because you couldn't feel it, but my mother used to put it in the middle of my tongue and give me a drink of water, and I suppose it got washed down.

You had to be very careful not to drop a lung-healer because you'd could never find it again.

I lost one once, and Margaret got full value out of it:

"Ooh! He's dropped a lung-healer! He's dropped a lung-healer!" Luckily there was one left, right at the bottom of the bag, and after the grim warning, "Drop that one, and I'll drop you!" I managed to get it down.

I don't know who made these near- microscopic lung-healers. Perhaps Mrs Smith made them? After all, she used to go into a corner behind the counter and do something before she handed over the toffee-bag. That didn't bother me so much as what happened when somebody brought a jug to the off-licence for a pint of beer. Mrs Smith would go behind a sort of display shelf and bend down, and you heard this trickling sound, and then she came out with the jug full ...

We had a big stone sarsparella bottle my mother used as a hot-water bottle in the front bedroom. In the back bedroom, (you know, where we nearly got killed during the blitz), my Dad used the oven-plate wrapped in the News Chronicle to keep the ashes off the flock bed.

Two more medicines I remember - sold in small, tube-like bottles - were *Composition* and *Indian Brandee*. One of them - I forget which- was rather like a very sweet red ink, and I think one of them was to make you go to the lavatory and the other to stop you going when you had dye yer rear.

But they may both have been for the same thing for all I remember now. Sometimes I used to get sent for a little flat tin box of laxative tablets too, rather like the little boxes they used to put gramophone needles in.

I didn't like the laxative tablets, they looked like toffees, but they had an unpleasant, gritty taste.

I liked the little bottles best. We also got olive oil in a little tubular bottle, and when we had a cough, Mother used to warm it in front of the fire, pour the oil into the palm of her hand and then rub it on our backs and chests. I still tend to think of olive oil that way, and I find it a little bit strange to see people cooking with olive oil or pouring it over a salad.

We also used to drink a teaspoonful of warm olive oil when we had had a cough. We were never given castor oil, I don't know why, but I've tasted it since, and I've never been able to understand why it should have been singled out as having a particularly nasty taste. I haven't any doubts at all about the nastiest thing I've ever drunk. It was *Fenning's Fever Cure*. You got a teaspoonful of it, gagging and crying, and when you swallowed it it turned your tongue bitter as gall and all your throat sour, and set all your teeth on edge. I suppose you could get the same sort of effect by drinking really strong vinegar, but Fenning's Fever Cure had a poisonous, sickening after-taste that stayed with you for hours. It put my temperature up just to see a spoonful coming towards me.

I don't know who *Fenning* was, but he must have been a sadistic old fiend. The only excuse I can think of for my mother is that, where medicine was concerned, she was a bit simple. She wasn't alone. There was a funny idea, current then, that a tarboiler helped you to get rid of your cold; all standing round with sore eyes sucking in the fumes.

Talking about colds, that was something else that I didn't much enjoy: having your temperature taken.

So far I expect I have given the impression that we never had a doctor. But we did. After all, you had to be born.

As a matter of fact we had the doctor to end all doctors. He used to drive up in a pony and trap, overhanging the sides, and there you were lying in bed, and you heard this Irish voice, untouched by about forty years of Lancashire life, rumbling "Whorr is he?" up the stairs.

Then there he was, at any rate, filling the whole bedroom, and shaking his thermometer at you. In those days, nobody in the working-class had a thermometer of their own. And a GP couldn't go round shoving his thermometer up people's rear-ends because it would have been both unhygienic and rude. So he put it in your mouth, and between patients, he would sterilise his thermometer in some antiseptic fluid or other which burned like fire when you got it on the tender membranes under your tongue, where you were told to put it.

"Ooooh! Aaagghhh!"

"Keep still now, will ye? Are ye a softie or something?"

"Oooooh...aaaagh....ooooh..."

"His pulse is a bit fast, his temperature a bit on the high side but nothing to worry about now, and Oi'll give ye a prescription for the pink bottle, three teaspoonsful a day. And *the top of the morning to ye*."

Compared with Fenning's Fever Cure, the pink bottle tasted like Vimto. You had to go to the chemist's to get the pink bottle "made up". There were several other colours, for example "the red bottle," "the brown bottle," "the yellow bottle" and so on. The chemist wrapped the big, flattish bottles up tightly in white paper so that you couldn't see what kind of bottle the doctor had given you until you got home, but most people were too curious to wait until they got home and tore off a little strip of the covering to see what they had got, and besides, they wanted to join in the discussion.

"Ee! he's given me another yellow bottle!" (Much clicking of tongues). And I've told him much and more. That yellow bottle doesn't do for me...It gives me palpitation. I'll have to see him about that. Ee! He never listens..."

"It looks like he's put me on the green bottle this time, I haven't tried that before. He's always given me the brown bottle. I haven't had the green bottle before."

"Oh, I have. It's a good bottle that. It's strong, mind you. And it's very bitter. I always have a toffee ready to take the taste away afterward..."

"Now, I like the blue bottle best. It stops a cough just like that. But he's put me on the tablets. I don't know why."

"What colour are they?"

"I haven't got the top off the box yet..."

"No., well, it looks to me like them little blue pills. I'd buy a bottle of Composition to take with them if I were you. I had to stop taking them. They gave me waterbrash...

(Prescription tablets were another thing, of course, and seemed to be made specifically for the patient in question. It actually used to say on the box "The Tablet", so you asked for them, rather pompously, by surname, i.e. 'The Clayborough Tablet, please ').

I sat on the bench next to my mother, kicking my legs and listening, until our name was called and we walked all the way home up Johnny Wraith Broo with the bottle still wrapped in its mystery.

Mother cut the white cover off the bottle of medicine. It was purple. Mother made a face.

"Just run next door for me, will you, Arthur," she told me, "And get a little bottle of Indian Brandee..."

A Good Cath'o'licking

We trooped into Andy Cusack's study, looking as innocent and puzzled as we could. We may not have been altogether innocent, but puzzled we were. Connell was great at it, real altar-boy stuff, but Nobby had a naturally delinquent face and stance which evened things out a bit. Patch looked earnest and bewildered.

How I looked I couldn't say, but for once the puzzlement was real. We hadn't been caught red handed, we never were. All the same we got more than a bit worried when Andy opened a drawer and pulled out his *totenschlager* , a thick black length of leather . Where he got it from I can't imagine. It didn't look like the sort of thing you might find in an illustrated school equipment catalogue. He threw back the right hand fold of his cape across his shoulder. He strutted about like that a lot, headmasterly, to show off his red satin lining, but as we weren't much good as an admiring audience, this time it was probably to give himself more freedom of action.

"Line up!"

We shuffled into a line and held out our hands.

"This isn't for anything particular," he told us, "It's for your general attitude for the past few weeks."

We got six each, which doesn't sound so bad, but when he had hit you three times on the same hand with his cosh, your whole arm went dead up to the elbow .

At least he was cool and crisp about it, not like Father Joe who came at you like the *Flail of the Lord* , or

Father Purcell ("Poice") whose sadism deserves another chapter on its own. Anyway, it's *getting* one.

When, a lot later on, I was studying to be a teacher myself (licensed, in those days, if not to kill, at least to twist little boys' arms up their backs), I told the Reader in Education (Owd Dobbin) about Poice, and he was horrified. He said he ought to have been handed over to the police. But the legend was that Poice had been a policeman himself, a Dublin cop, and kicked off the force for being too violent (in Ireland!).

So he had had no other option but being a priest, God help us all.

(I can't say He did, much, but then He'd be on Poice's side, wouldn't He?)

"And before you leave ," Andy told us, "you are all in detention next Wednesday afternoon." We went out of the old house where he had his study hurt and angry.

"Detention? I've never *been* off the bloody board of honour," Larry grumbled.

You had to get a weekly average of four to miss monthly detention, - five was the highest mark - and he had never been under that in his school career. That was probably the most infuriating thing about him for the staff. He shouldn't have been at the top of the class in everything, or as they saw it, anything. But *he* wasn't anybody's idea of a teacher's pet, to say nothing of Nobby or me, though we didn't have anything like Patch's brains. You couldn't pin Larry down, he was just too far ahead of the game .

On Monday mornings, whatever priest we happened to have for the first period had the job of asking us whether we had performed our Sunday duties and - believe it or not - *caning* the ones who hadn't , and/or giving them a two for behaviour, which more or less condemned you to monthly detention.

Since we all lived in nearby towns (and "pretty how towns" they were, too, Accrington, Burnley, Darwen (like me) Great Harwood, even Rawtenstall and Nelson), it was a question of owning up, which most boys couldn't, or (for some reason) wouldn't, dodge. Probably lack of moral courage.

This Monday, however, it was "Spud" Murphy's turn . Our morning to howl.

The roll-call ensured.

"John Cassidy" (Cassidy was a quiet, neat Burnley boy).

"Mass and Communion, Father."

"Good boy!   Terence Frayne?"

(I liked Frayne, he look a bit like a bear, and in fact Tony Connell had invented the terrible pun for him "Bruin T. ("Brewing tea") Frayne) .

"Mass an' Benediction,"

"*Father.!.*" Spud Murphy scowled at him. (It sounded like "Feyther" the way he said it. He was an Irish as Paddy's proverbial pig.)

"Uh, Mass-an'-Benediction, *Father* ." Bruin just missed saying "*Feyther*" which would have meant a whack with the cane.

" Bert?." Bert(rand) Ledwick , big brown eyes, freckles, violin, was a special kid from a right holy home in Accrington. I remember visiting Bert, who was obviously *en route* for the Jesuits, and being confronted in the parlour by a vast, signed, photograph of the Pope.

" Mass, Communion and Benediction, Father!"

"Good, good."

Incidentally, they caught ol'Spud at Birkenhead later, with 'incriminating letters' in his socks. It was in the *Northern Daily Telegraph*.

"West!"

Bobby West was an all right kid, I think his dad was a Blackburn fireman or something. Anyway, I gathered from the joshing in class that Spud was a regular visitor at their house for tea and wads. But that meant that he daren't lie.

"Uh, went a walk, Father!"

This was the usual euphemism for "didn't go!".

Another one was "Overslept, Father." Now this put Murphy in a bit of a spot. He didn't want to give up his tea and wads. But he had to give him a whack, or a two. It was a whack, but not a very convincing one. He once whacked *me* with my own metal ruler what I had just paid sixpence for at Woolworth's, and bent it over my outstretched hand, to the joy of my sympathetic classmates.

"Wilkinson!"

Spud looked aggressively at Patch, daring him to lie, but it wasn't a bit of use.

"Mass and Communion, Father!" he lied. ("I thought of putting Benediction in as well, but I didn't want to overdo it.")

Murphy looked as though he'd like to rough Larry up a bit and get at the truth, but he could only glare.

"Noblett!"

Nobby looked sheepish.

"I went a walk, Father…" He held out a limp, yellow-fingered hand, as the square, cassocked figure rolled up the passageway at him.

Me next.

How did I end up in this mass/mess?

Well, whilst my Dad was the world's least satisfactory Catholic, my mother must have " turned Catholic" for him and agreed under pressure from the local priests to have her children brought up Catholic. It must have been Mother who was involved in this because apart from being a great Dad, he was about the most unsatisfactory Catholic who ever lived.

I imagine it all went something like this. As a young single working-man, Dad got a lodging with a family called Shannon – the name speaks volumes – and they found a wife called Teresa for him in an Irish orphanage.

There was an old photo of her in a drawer for years, and my mother must have told me who it was. Apart from what looked to me like a crooked finger-nail, she looked fairly normal in a sort of Georgian dress with her hair up. I never got to know what she died of the infamous Spanish Flu, probably, but as my older sister was christened Teresa after her, some older Catholics wrongly assumed that she was a stepdaughter.

Whilst my Mother took her "conversion" fairly seriously, my Dad, apart (presumably) from his first marriage, never set foot inside a Catholic – or for that matter any – church, except when my two sisters got married in non-Catholic churches to non-Catholic husbands.

The story goes that Father Farrelly, a young newcomer , fresh from Ireland,, making the local rounds, slipped in through the front door and came face to face with Dad who asked him:

"Did tha' knock?"

"Well, no…"

"Aye, well get outside and knock if tha' wants to come in!"

"But I'm your spiritual father!"

"Ah've only got one feyther, an' he lives in Hacking Street! So if of tha's wants to come in, another time, knock…."

My mother's resigned comment was "Well, I might have been taking a bath…." (In our (leaky) tin bath on the hearth rug…)

When, many years later, in a different house, we had a visit from an exceptionally saintly priest, Father Walsh, who sat on the sofa with us, leaving his hat on the sideboard,

Dad couldn't resist putting the hat on and making silly faces.

It was agonising, for us, especially when it became clear that Father Walsh could see Dad acting the goat through a looking-glass over the fireplace, but he contented himself with remarking mildly: "Your husband seems to be something of a comedian, Mrs Clayborough..."

We didn't know where to look...

Otherwise we were fairly normal Catholics as far as it went which wasn't all that far. But a consequence was that my two sisters and I ended up going to St. Joseph's Catholic school in Darwen, and that I topped it off by attending St Mary's College in Blackburn.

And so there I was now, with my hand out, paying the price, perhaps, for Dad's impromptu comedy routine.

I can't remember getting the strap or cane until I got to St. Mary's College up Shear Brow in Blackburn. where canings were a regular part of the curriculum unless you were a right teacher's pet.

There was an interesting difference in the styles and equipment. Joe, (Father Stuart, but 'Joe', or occasionally 'Father Joe' to us) who took us for French, used to line up the ones who couldn't conjugate *devoir* or whatever at the side of the classroom. (There was generally a pretty healthy queue.) Then when the bell rang, he stood at the door giving everybody a couple on the flat of the hand as we trooped out for lunch.

Spud Murphy made it more of a game.

"Lol" Patton was an ice cold bugger whose spectacles glinted as he sliced the palm of your hand with all his skinny energy.

The headmaster, Andy Cusack, as mentioned, hit you with a thick leather cosh that deadened all your arm for about ten minutes.

But the cream of the crop, to put it that way, was Purcell, sparse red hair and broken teeth, who really enjoyed his thrashings. When he had hit you on the tips of your fingers, he'd make you but your hand palm upward on the desk instead of nursing it. "Let it stew in its own jouice!" he'd growl and as he went past he might have a second slash at the upturned hand

"Leaving ship!"

"Ah, e—egredior uh....

Whack!...

His other speciality was pulling and flicking the end of your nose to produce a red spot; I remember one kid had a polyp up his nose and blood poured down to the floor. Didn't discourage the practice, though. Took more than that. His relationship to the body was summed up with strange, literally chest-thumping declarations; 'Worms will eat *this*!', and occasionally, 'Only got one lung, y'know.'

The only one who didn't whack or even give twos was Father John (Cowell), plump, well-shaved, swept-back silver hair, who sat down, deposited two mint imperials (always two) on the desk in front of him and ate them at carefully timed intervals. As I remember it, that was *all* he did. He never got up to whack you, and couldn't be bothered writing you down.

But a Catholic education was, you may be surprised to hear, more than just about finding excuses to beat us. There were, of course, the retreats, those religious days when you *had* to be religious. We could during retreats walk about in 'contemplation', or in pairs muttering very quietly to each other. In the classroom , this devotional time was devoted to the reading of the numerous CTS

('Catholic Truth Society') pamphlets provided. If you were brave, you could slip a comic inside these, in fact, Yankee comics were the perfect size.

I remember one pamphlet being particularly popular, though, it's own right. *The Life of Father James Doyle* was almost as good as any comic, specifically the part about how he used to carve the Holy Name of Jesus on his chest with a penknife.

Our running joke question was :

"Did he dot the 'J' and stab himself?"

Of course, nobody dared ask any of the priests that.

The other running joke, also a question, I remember was caused by Father Joe's pious intonation: "Grant that I may be with thee always and then do with me what thou wilt."

Begging of course, the question: "What the hell could you *do* with Joe?"

Alas, these deep religious matters remain unanswered.

Scruffy Flower

Halfway down. A hanging wall,
Rushing roughbacked from my eye.
Falling. A wild waterfall.
Out of the kingdom of the sky.

Hanging, I scraped acquaintanceship-
A tuft of grass and a scruffy flower.
Leaning against its ragged hip
They sweetened all that granite tower

And that I want to know is: Why
They looked so bright against the stone,
Or whether anybody but I
Would have loved them,
living there alone

In't Bible

So I recall looking down from the choir into the well of the church in May listening to the strong rhetorical bay of Father Lineen the yellow Gothic vulture in the pulpit, followed by the great boom of the litany from the faithful, all the more faithful for being non-resident Irish:

"Tower of Ivory, PRAY FOR US"

"Tower of David, PRAY FOR US"

"Mystical Rose, PRAY FOR US"

"Ark of the Covenant, PRAY FOR US"

The candles, the flowers the lights, the little garlanded girls, the white frocks and veils. Also the priest on his way round the church in his gold robes holding up the monstrance and the clouds of incense wafting up like fairy floss.

And Maurice "Snuffer" Durkin with a long neck and that like long pole wi' a snuffer on the end and a taper stuck in the top trying to light rows and rows of candles on the altar watched by hundreds of eyes. It wasn't much, but it was all the fun there was... I thought that with that neck, he looked like a snuffer himself.

Every now and then I read a bit of Bible, most of it on loose sheets of rice paper scattered in my Dad's drawer with old shaving brushes, nuts and bolts and stuff. Mother was afraid he had been using it to stuff out the front of his cap and that was why we never had any luck, but it turned out that he only used twists of *Empire News*, yellowed with age. Or maybe it was *News of The World*. It changes with each telling.

There was still about half of the Old Testament left. I couldn't understand why people in't Bible did what they did. Like, these angels in Sodom, and all these old and young men who called unto Lot "Where are the men which came into thee this night? Bring them out to us that we may *know* them."

I couldn't quite understand why the Lord wanted to destroy this city, just because the men wanted to get to *know* these angels.

I liked *Samson* best, anyway, being all strong and doing all those nutty things like tying burning torches to the tails of three hundred foxes. (Imagine just *catching* three hundred foxes…)

My Dad told me that he had seen the pillars that Samson pulled down while he was in Palestine during the Great War. Don't ask me what he was doing in Palestine. I didn't ask him, but he wouldn't have known anyway. I don't suppose anybody did, including the generals and 'Lord Joige'. My Dad seemed proud at having had three general court marshals, so I was too, a bit, though I'd no idea what it meant. I was even proud of them giving Dad three days rations and a donkey and telling him to find his own way back to the coast. I mean, it showed that they relied on his judgment and his own "invisible initiative" or something like that.

The Olympia Entry

I don't live in Darwen, now, or even in England. But my sister Teresa's old pal Ruth does, and we correspond. I wrote recently to ask Ruth if the Olympia entry was still there, a dark, covered passageway from the main road at the side of the cinema that led down some steps into a sort of yard and then up some more steps to Sunny Bank Street and Red Earth Road . I had vivid memories of the Olympia entry, because our little gang was once chased down there by a much bigger, rougher and ruggeder one from Radford. We considered making a last stand there with our little bamboo rods with flags on, against a mob armed among other things with splintered pick-handles. Happily we chickened out (or I might not be writing this) and circled back to find that all our bonfire wood, piled up on John Houghton's kitchen roof, had gone.

The answer I got by post was that not only was there no longer an Olympia entry, there wasn't any Olympia either. The Olympia which (so I heard) could seat three thousand souls (if souls *need* seats, that is) was easily the biggest cinema in Darwen (there were, let's see, five, including the Albert Hall (true) and the Public Hall, known locally as the Laugh-and-Scratch. A rival cinema, the Palladium, used to trumpet in the local Advertiser: "Follow the crowds to the Palladium!" But in our late teens when there was no Sunday cinema, Alan and I usually followed the girls, in their two-piece costumes, trooping up in our raglan overcoats and pork pie hats, (which we had to remove) to the Olympia's Sunday night "go-as-you –please" concerts, along with the other 2,998 souls, with a hundred per cent local talent to support.

No, not quite, there would occasionally be a glamorous visiting personality On one occasion during the war, it was a Canadian newsreader who had become famous for reading the news on the BBC faster than anybody else, so he came on stage and read something or other like a machine gun. How we all laughed and clapped! The high point of these concerts was reached when we got enough money together to send Archie Lewis to London to sing with Billy Cotton's Band. He turned up looking very handsome in a blue blazer and a shining black face. None of us 3000 souls had ever seen anything like that before, neither the blue blazer nor the face. He sang *Carry Me Back To Old Virginny*, though Kingston Town would probably have been more like it.

If I'm not mistaken, Archie turned up again some time later, after he had sung with Billy Cotton's Band, to thank an overflow audience (3002 souls) and collect another fare to London. As a matter of fact I think we sent him back to London a good few times. We felt we had a certain stake in his success, though he didn't really belong to us. He was after all only a bird of passage, not like the great West Indian cricketer Leary Constantine, who stayed on in Accrington so long that they had to make him mayor.

The songs in the go-as-you-please contest were accompanied by John Reed's Band, apart from the girls who sang serious stuff to the piano like One Fine Day From Madam Butterfly

("and when he reaches the brow of the hillock...") and Bless This House (I mistakenly thought the words were "Bless these walls so firm and stout, Keeping one another out".)

One contestant who brought the house down was a young man with a limp who sang Three Minutes Of Heaven ("...and then, God Bless You, Good Night!...") We all felt sorry for him and clapped and clapped. (nobody whistled in those days), and if I'm not mistaken, he won.

I saw him later on in Blackburn without any limp. It was a good gimmick, though.

One Sunday they had a competition where you had to beat John Reed's Band with a song they couldn't play (I don't mean Beethoven's Fifth or even his First.). Somebody baffled John Reed *and* his Band (and for that matter all of us) by asking them to play "Playboy, Play Around!" They asked the challenger to hum a bit of it but he couldn't, and after a great deal of discussion which , if I'm not mistaken, spilled over to the following Sunday's concert, it was publicly announced that there was no such song.

We were always sorry when the lights went on and the tip-up seats were tipped up again, and we all tipupped out into Bolton Road and followed the crowds to the Circus. Not the "send in the clowns" sort of circus, just the town centre, where now and then policemen stood outside the *Millstone* (or whatever the pub was called) directing such traffic as there was, while Bella shouted insults at him, with her long white hair flying about. The story was that this strange old woman had once been jilted by a policeman and gone a bit doolally, so she stood there shouting abuse at any poor constable who turned up on point duty (before the traffic lights were put up by the mayor) and the police were given strict instructions never to interfere with her.

"You rotten little bugger!"

"You bloody little rat!"

She would shout things like that. No obscenities as far my recollection goes, which isn't far these days. "Bugger" wasn't an obscenity then; and "little" didn't mean "small" it meant "young", so "Little George" could be six foot two, in which case he would be a policeman, because there wasn't anybody else in Darwen who was six foot two, except Vin Humphreys , and he doesn't count. He once got three out of a hundred in a geometry exam. Admittedly, he was a lot better looking than either Alan or me, but. still, three out of a hundred. Not much, is it?

Untitled 5

Here I am, at the official end of my youth,
thin as a wolf after a hard winter
two thousand feet up in the rain-softened air
with my roughened feet resting on a rock splinter.

This is a seminal country, where sensations
come singly, like cut flowers in Japan:
you acquire a taste for the duller pleasures,
and body and soul become part of the same man.

Like the long-forgotten tendons in your heels,
some frail strand in the brain aches and grows strong
with crossing rock, and far in the distance feels
the enormous importance of bird song.

Following Girls

I grew up at a time when girls were different from boys. They were separated at school by big iron railings with spikes on them, rather like the ones round the rhinoceros compound at the zoo. (The last time we were at the zoo, my small daughter looked with awe at a small cat washing its paws inside a huge iron fence with a space of about two feet between the bars, probably intended for elephants or rhinos. "Can it get out, Dad?" she whispered).

I had two sisters, so I was over the worst, but that fence did make you more curious about what they were up to, which, at playtime anyway, seemed to be the endless singing of a song beginning: " The rain, the rain, the rain comes down..."

about which girl was interested in which boy. The boys used to crowd up to the rhinoceros bars to hear their names being called out, but mine never was as far as I know, which isn't all that far.

I went on to another school where there were no girls at all, not even on the other side of the bars, not even to talk to in front of the guards. There was a parallel place down in town, though, where there was nothing else but girls and they dressed in dark green with little Robin Hood caps on. You used to sit behind them on the tram. I fell in love with one who lived up behind the park in a posh house, and had a very pretty face with a rather nice nose and sexy, slightly bowed legs in thick brown stockings. I only ever spoke to her once and was rather frightened when it turned out that she knew my name and even used it. I moved about on a cushion of air, rather like wearing these new jogging shoes, perhaps, for the best part of a week; but I was scared of meeting her again because I didn't know what might happen if I did.

And yet I wanted to find out. I'm not all that sure what teenagers are like now, although I have had enough of them to have some idea. Not as different as they are supposed to be, I would guess. Anyway, in those days, most young people preferred the whole thing to be a castle in the air built on a smile or a hello. I mean, your homework took you nearly all night.

When I was about sixteen, like the other lads in my class, I only wore my school cap where we had to, for about a hundred yards to and from the school. On the tram home, you felt (quite wrongly) that you couldn't be told from those who went to work and were part of the real world.

I used to wear, at one stage anyway, a grubby "military" raincoat, all leather buttons and straps. The left side was stained pink with the red dye from a school book running down it in the rain. A geography book it was. One day, as I was getting off at the Circus, a perky little conductress with a blonde bubblecut caught hold of my sleeve.

"What are you doing tonight?" she asked me.

It was the moment of truth when you showed what you were made of, but before I could do more than gulp ("My God, she thinks I'm grown up...") a chubby second former with his school cap over his ear came clattering down the stairs dragging his satchel and chummily asked me if I had any homework.

The bubblecut head retreated inside with a bagful of pennies. I tried to avoid any tram she might be on for a week or two, but I was probably more relieved than otherwise. She would have been too much for me. And I certainly hadn't got a bagful of pennies.

One of my school pals, Patch, who had a blond moustache and a Home Guard uniform, used to tell us about undoing blouses on the market ground at

Accrington after late night dances. Perhaps he could have managed her, but I doubt it. It was nearly all lies.

At weekends, Alan and I used to follow girls

We weren't all that interested in actually catching any. We just trailed after any likely-looking bunch of bright swagger coats and handbags, staying about fifty to a hundred yards behind. The girls - usually there would be two of them - always knew they were being followed, but never let on. They didn't seem to be as nervous about it as we were. We would pick up the trail of one of the couples we regularly followed and dog them up and down Blackburn Road, round the Market Hall, booking for the pictures and so on.

They would be wearing two-piece tweed suits or swinging calf-length coats in bright colours which made them easy to follow. They never wore hats, and had their hair curled at the ends, either outwards, or inwards in a "page-boy" style. I liked the outwards style best. I don't know why; perhaps I didn't fancy pageboys.

We would be wearing pork-pie hats and long "raglan" overcoats with check patterns on, flapping open to show our sports coats and slacks. Alan was rather better-looking and much better groomed than I was, but he nearly always had a prominent boil on the back of his neck with a sticking-plaster over it. I only ever had one boil - but I am jumping the gun.

On Saturday nights we went to the pictures. Occasionally we were lucky enough to sit close to some girls, but in those days, going to the pictures was a bit like going to church. Hankypanky wasn't tolerated, even if we had been cheekier than we were. Unless, that is, you could afford balcony prices, or even a box. We couldn't.

I remember once trying to show off - at the Palladium, I think it was - during a vampire bat film with Lionel

Atwill. The vampire bat in the film had a fox's head, and as I used to read animal books at what old Tommy Oldham called *The Bloodsucker's Library*, I could see that it was really a fruit bat that was being used. Rather more loudly than was necessary, I informed Alan: "That isn't a vampire bat. It's a fruit bat!"

Even more loudly and indignantly came the swagger-coated feminine chorus from the next seats:"Shurrr-ooop!" So much for scientific information.

After the pictures we used to walk round the park in the dark eating sixpennyworths of chips, each chip coaxed out in turn through a hole in the warm, smelly bundles of newspaper.

We talked about girls of course, cheerfully mixing together film stars and the local girls we followed. They were all just as remote from us.

We used to compete with one another inventing the most exciting idea, which girl, dressed in what, would you like to be with, and where. That sort of thing. Meanwhile we ambled happily on under the lamps, each with his lukewarm bundle of chips. We couldn't possibly have been happier on a tropical island underneath the palm trees with Veronica Lake in a sarong, or - what was marginally more likely - walking through the park with Joyce P. or Mary T. in a fawn lambswool two-piece costume.

On Sundays, after church, we used to follow girls through Sunnyhurst Wood, usually in a big circle, coming out by the bottom gate where we went in. Like Omar Khayyam.

One Sunday, however, the inevitable happened. We were following Joyce P. and Mary T. (we knew their names but that was all) and it was pretty clear right away that they were up to something. Instead of ignoring us as usual, they turned round every so often.

We even caught a smile or two, or thought we did. We were tingling with nerves. We both wanted to turn back, I think, but we couldn't. Not now.

We shuffled out of the wood at the top gate, more and more slowly, pork-pie hats shadowing our faces. Sunday strollers thinned out, and soon there was nobody and nothing to hide behind at all.

Round the side of the reservoir they walked, and there, on the steep grassy hillside, they sat down deliberately with their little dog racing round them, quite clearly waiting for *us*. It was God knows how many years ago, but even now, I could show you the exact spot.

We turned pale. We stared hard at one another. We breathed faster. "What are we going to do?" we muttered. This wasn't at all the same thing as walking round the park with our sixpennorths. It was *real*. We had actually *clicked*, and we didn't quite like it. But we trailed nearer, bowed down by the weight of our raglan overcoats.

Suddenly the little dog had a go at us. It ran round us, barking, shrewdly realised that we were completely harmless, and started jumping up muddily at us. The girls laughed, and one of them said,

"I think he's welcoming you!"

We looked at the pretty faces and sat down. We already knew which sides to sit on. We had got to the end of the rainbow and those few, first, terribly embarrassing, magical minutes began when very ordinary lads like us found themselves struggling to put up a good show against a feeling of not having much to show off with.

They were both very pretty. Joyce, who was on the tall side, and hers was the side I sat down on, had big dreamy brown eyes, long dark-brown hair and a nice figure. She looked a bit like Gene Tierney, I thought.

Just being pretty was all they needed. Come to think of it, we needed to be a bit prettier too, but there wasn't much to be done about that, either then or since.

They didn't make goo-goo eyes at us or smile with their tongues between their teeth or anything like that. *What we talked about, I don't know.* I didn't even know five minutes after we had left them, after walking them home.

Talking to girls naturally led to going out with girls, but apart from standing them a glass of sarsaparilla in Woods's toffee shop a Sunday or two later, that was about all that happened. I only remember talking to Joyce once later, and that was when I had my boil. It was all the boils of my teens rolled into one. It was on the left side of my head, which swelled up like a football. It hurt a lot and must have looked terrible. I felt as though my whole face, my mouth, nose and left eye, were being dragged over to one side. I looked like a Picasso.

I got off school, and my mother made a medical expedition to a local health stores and came back with a big bitter black bottle of "herbal mixture". I had to drink it three times a day and it would do me a world of good.

I managed to survive, largely because I had had a lot of training with Fennings Fever Cure, the most horrible concoction ever to enter a human mouth, consisting, as far as I could tell, of equal parts of sulphuric acid, gall, and concentrated vinegar. It sort of melted your teeth.

I must admit that the boil was gone within a week. Because of the herbal mixture, my mother said.

While it was still at its peak, however, I found I couldn't stand being in the house any longer, and I took my library books back.

On the way out I met Joyce, also carrying books, and we walked down School Street together, looking like Quasimodo and Esmerelda. If I had climbed on top of the Coop Meeting Rooms, holding her over my head and shouting "Sanctuary! Sanctuary!" it might have led somewhere, but as it was, I could feel in my bones that this was goodbye.

She looked particularly wonderful of course that afternoon, a soft brown scarf matching her big brown eyes. She chatted about having got a place at a university, keeping the eyes to the front.

I had lost her. The fact that I had never actually *won* her in the first place made it easier to bear, perhaps, and afterwards I went for a romantic walk in Boldventure Park, this time without any chips, and composed a poem, something about her red-brown peat stream eyes if my memory doesn't fail me. It's at the back of a drawer somewhere but I think I could still find it if it is ever needed.

I suppose that nondescript-looking lads like me usually move on from following girls to talking to girls. At any rate they did then. I don't know what they move on to now, but I feel a bit sorry for anybody who gets there too quick because I don't think you should open your presents before Christmas.

What mattered about talking to girls was quantity, not quality, getting plenty of time in.

When I think about those endless summer evenings, two things seem to run together for me. One was reading trashy library books like *The Prisoner of Zenda*, and *She*, sitting in the park on the steps of the war memorial surrounded by rosebushes and great black-painted iron chains with knobs on, reading until the print swam in front of my eyes in the twilight.

On one side of the war memorial it said THEIR NAME LIVETH FOR EVERMORE, and on the other side it said LEST WE FORGET.

The other teen-age thing I remember about girls is standing on our front steps talking to Mary P., the girl from next door but one, leaning on the low side wall. It used to have bits of soda on top to clean the wall when it rained. After a couple of hours, you needed the wall, and at my present age I would have to have something with soda in it too.

Finally, our faces were just blurs in the dusk, which didn't much matter as far as my face was concerned, but she was worth looking at, with a small, neat head and curly hair and a long neck. God only knows what she looks like now, but the chances are that she is still a lot prettier than me.

We must have found plenty of things to talk about, but from all that muttering and laughing and whispering, I can't remember a single thing either of us said.

No. I tell a lie. Just one. One of the boys in her class at the grammar school kept unfastening the shoulder straps of her gymslip, and she had had to sew them up. I remember wanting to punch his head for doing it. Perhaps because I wanted to do it myself.

After a whole summer of talking, we found ourselves arranging to go for a walk together. It doesn't sound like much when you put it that way, but my first parachute jump turned out to be a lot less nerve-wracking.

The walk itself wasn't very exciting. I remember where we went, though, and one curious thing that happened.

I didn't smoke; the nearest I had got to cigarettes was going for a packet of Star for my Dad and getting the cigarette-cards, (A.R.P. tips and that). But I bought a packet of "Black Cat" (I think they were called) so I could offer her one. I must have thought it was the sort of sophisticated thing they did on the pictures.

To be quite honest, I had once tried to smoke myself at the pictures in the dark, and I was so worried about being recognised if I struck a match, that I tried to light a cigarette while holding it underneath the seat. Later on, when I was old enough to take Dad to the pictures and even smoke a pipe inside, as you could then, he complained that when I lit the damned thing the flames threw shadows up the cinema walls.

I forgot all about the cigarettes until we were walking along a path high on the moors between drystone walls. It was about six in the evening, the sun was still high and there were skylarks singing everywhere in the blue sky. Suddenly I pulled out my pack of *Black Cat* or *Kensitas* or whatever it was and asked her if she would like a cigarette.

"No, thank you," she said. "I don't smoke."

"Neither do I," I said, and threw the packet, *still unopened,* over a wall into a field.

We walked on in silence. I can see now that she must have thought I wasn't all there, and it dampened things down for a while. The only other thing I can remember was that she told me - right up at the top of Darwen Tower, it was - that that was how you held a baby, not a girl. So something or other must have happened, but not much.

The next step in my sexual education was going dancing at the local Coop Hall and "over the Baths". where some months later an R.A.F. uniform (with those rough trousers that gnawed at your legs) helped to bridge the gap between overgrown schoolboy and factory girl. All that endless shuffling round with an occasional little skip to the *Dark Town Strutters Ball* and *American Patrol* and *In The Mood*.

I can only dimly imagine how boring it must have been for my partners, Doreen and Betty and Sheila and Mary and the other names I'm keeping to myself. But generally speaking they put up with my shuffle-and-skip good-humouredly, even when I stood on their golden shoes or got my brass buttons fast in their hair-do's. (At that time the fashionable style for girls, unbelievable as it sounds, was hair swept up into a pile on the crown of the head, *round a bread roll.* Gradually the dance would work its way up to the climax, the "Who's taking you home tonight" tune:

"Who's the lucky boy who's going your way,

To kiss you goodnight at your doorway..."

It was very important to be dancing with the right girl for that one, and there was a great deal of intrigue and jockeying for position.

My God, the miles I used to walk, "taking you home tonight".(Nobody ordinary had a car in those days and even extraordinary people hadn't any petrol.) Sometimes all the way to Blackburn and back, sometimes nearly to Bolton, or at least Watery Lane.

I don't know why, either. Of course, it was chemistry, your hormones and all that, but there was something else, a feeling that your life was on the move. Taking a girl home from a dance proved you were normal, you were in. It perked up your self-confidence as nothing else could, and for those of us who were still just kids at school when other chaps of our age were at work with real jobs, that was all-important.

What do you remember, all those years later? Floating along under the street lamps, with a girl's arm tucked under yours, and the last tram trailing past unheeded in a shower of blue sparks.

One week I took home an immensely tall girl a bit like an emu whose eyes seemed to be set rather low down on either side of a sharp little nose which she stuck in my cheek when she bent down to kiss me goodnight at the top of Watery Lane. That wasn't so bad. It could have been my eye.

The following week I took home a chubby little Land girl with a protruding tooth that cut my bottom lip. At the top of Watery Lane that was, as well. The week after I was cuddling a girl with shadows under her eyes and tobacco breath; and the week after that a bouncy grocer's daughter at the side of a nightwatchman's brazier.

Once I walked all round Sunnyhurst Wood with a pretty, experienced blonde girl who got more and more fed up with me for about an hour and a half. She had already had a number of satisfying relationships with G.I.'s, and the more she harped on them, the more she brought out my own total lack of glamour. We parted in mutual frustration, but I hope she finally made it to San Berdoo or Wilshire Boulevard and that it was all she ever hoped for.

Looking back on what I've been saying about following girls, it strikes me all over again how much legwork there was in getting to know the opposite sex, following them, dancing with them or going for walks and then seeing them home, over the moors past the Farmer's Den to the Belmont Road, up Bull Hill, round Rocky Brook and Tockholes, down Sandy Lane, all the way to Blackburn for a squeeze through a swagger coat and a raglan, and a peck under a pork pie hat, something to dream about all the way home. Was it the real thing this time, something to set off against the "What time do you call this, then?" routine when you actually got home at last to be told off.

"Sorry, Mother, I missed the last tramcar."

"Tramcar? What? From the Baths? It's only a ten-minute walk."

"I had to see somebody home. You needn't sit up and wait."

"I'm not leaving the door open all night. You never know who might come in."

Somebody might have come in and stolen one of our painted plates, like *Storm coming up over Douglas, Isle of Man*. Somebody might have stolen my fish-and-chip supper, cold as it was. Somebody might even have stolen my mother.

Nobody ever did that, but a few years later, somebody stole my heart. That's another story; but if *mine* was stolen, somebody will certainly be after yours.

He who knows nothing

He who knows nothing, is no less wise

than bruised and injured violets' eyes

or any berry-bearing bush

under the onslaughts of a thrush.

I read about Napoleon's wars

by windows raindrops filled with stars,

and Cicero's Pro Roscio

filled my head with grass and snow.

Smoking

My Dad smoked ten *Star* a day. That was just about what he could afford, I know because I was the one who slipped over the low wall which ran down between Smith's off-license and our house (which the Smiths owned). The cigarettes were in silver paper inside an orange packet with a gold star on the front. I got the cigarette card (ARP tips etc.,) The only one I can remember showed somebody shovelling up an incendiary bomb with an unbelievably long-handled shovel of a kind nobody had, not even the ARP wardens.

You hear about the enormous value of complete sets of these cards in good condition today, they seem to "be worth a small fortune, but the ones school kids like me got were never "in pristine condition", just grubby, because we used to play down-on-your--knees games with them, flicking cards at one standing against a wall ("knock-down") or sliding on to a horizontal card ("slitch-on").

A small (or medium) fortune would come in handy today if I could find any at the back or bottom of a dresser drawer lined with pages from old *John Bull*s or *Empire News,* along with the ubiquitous bits of rice-paper Bible.

I can't remember actually smoking cigarettes, though I remember experimenting secretly and sinfully of all places in the balcony of the Olympia cinema (you were allowed to smoke at the pictures in those days and there were even little brass ashtrays on the backs of the seats).

I can even remember trying to light a cigarette *under the seat* but for some reason it didn't work unless you sucked at one end. I just gave up after Father Walsh or "some other big (clerical) cheese" explained to me in the confessional that smoking cigarettes *wasn't actually a sin.*

In my lascivious teens I once got pretty Mary Plumb to agree to go for a romantic walk and bought a packet of *Black Cat* (I think they were called) so I could offer her one sophisticatedly, and on the way to Sunnyhurst Wood, in the evening sun, I pulled out these fags and offered her one, and she said "I don't smoke", and as I didn't either, I just said, " I don't, either", and threw the pack - *unopened* even for the fag-card – over a wall into a field.

I expect she looked at me a bit sideways, but we must have been romantic enough to walk all the way up to the Tower, where I made what was as far as I can remember my first feeble and fumbling attempt at a romantic embrace. "That's how you hold a baby" she told me.

Sadly, perhaps, we never actually got round to holding one *together*.

I was in my twenties I think when I got as far as sucking on an old pipe of my Dad's (I must have liked the taste) until he got fed up with the sound of air whistling over tobacco-free tonsils. He bought me an ounce of Bruno Flake and I became a pipe-smoker for about ten years. My Dad once complained to my mother, that whilst we were watching a Randolph Scott in the Palladium, "Every time he lit his pipe, there were flames gooin' up the bloody walls".

Just after the war I got a job teaching English in Germany (I remember a dumbfounded soldier on the train asking me "Do you mean, you're *living wi'Jerries*?"). Wandering into a German tobacconists' with my pipe , I asked for "Uh, pfeifentobakk" and I was met with the customary radiant smile and the question "*Amerikanische, Englische, oder Holländische ?*"

He planked down three generous paper packages in different colours; but you soon discovered that they all contained the same old dried straw, at a time when smuggled cigarettes and Nescafe were used as money, and there were gunfights between smuggling gangs on the Bodensee.

I tried a German brand called "Golden Mixture" which I was assured by the affable tobacconist " didn't bite the tongue". He might have added, "It goes for the throat".

Fortunately my colleague Ronny's French wife worked in the American PX in Stuttgart, and I was supplied, for a mere pittance, with generous drums of *Prince Albert* ('in the can', of course) , *Edgeworth, Half and Half,* and even *Balkan Sobranie* .

When I took the family to Norway some years later, I began to tail off on tobacco, trotting along the Bergen-Nesttun road in preparation for the great *Ulriken Over (Bergen)* versus *Gråkollen Rundt (Trondheim)* race. I might add that Bergen collected ten thousand enthusiasts and won hands down.

I haven't smoked since.

The Tower; A Poem in Blank Verse

A: From Darwen Tower to the Northwest

The sky was grey, with rain on its mouth,

and a moistened wind forced its way round the tower.

Four small white crescents of bone showed where my hand clutched a pitted granite scroll.

Before me the earth fell to the fields then rose clearer, greener, across the valley;

the sky was level and grew vaguer with distance.

Under the tower, just beyond the soft clay paths writhing around the base,

harsh moor grass to spread, undulating at first,

brightening as it fell to a sudden hollow,

yellowing as it lifted in a short callous mane over a rise,

until it rolled to the left in a faded plateau.

This ended where a distant black hill began a flowing forward ridge,

above which the low cloud had a burned edge,

and the sun sent down it's seven only shafts;

but the border of the plateau filed up the valley,

overstepping the tawny path that toiled up past the tower

to sidle along the very edge of the moor,

plunged sullenly over the height to the masochistic meadows beneath.

Here the heather's dark was abruptly arrested,

dammed by a low wall on the valley floor,

and the gayer grass broke away, growing and swelling into a rise

insignificantly crowned by two handlike trees.

But beyond glowed even greener fields, and appropriately,

above them frank blue came through a white break.

Here the fall of land ceased and the far rise began

slowly to the far woods. The eye was held first by the

prim blind hedges dissecting the verdine,

then by one square field hanging brown stained

with black haycocks and studded with white lime heaps.

Big it went following a brown field and above it were the hazy woods,

dark to the sky's grey, striking a tilted and polished lake,

which started a snake of trees through the last visible meadows.

A ridge rose to the west, thrusting towards me a low hill,

down which a wood cascaded back to the climbing valley,

and burst along the floor to the right.

A low bar of cloud like a last ridge hung above this ridge-horizon,

making its faint fan of trees less distinct,

and in some fast instant of sunlight, an estuary gleamed.

The sunlight vanished, cutoff as by a guillotine,

as I went under the archway and resting my palm

against the inner wall which revolved with the spiral stairway,

I began the ascent.

The endless grey steps were set off in sixes by light of the sunset

which came through the Norman slits at intervals in the outer wall.

B: *The Tower*

Losing the sunlight as I entered,

For it failed at the doorway, cautiously

I placed a palm to the grey inner wall

And stood considering until I could see.

I felt no need for haste; if passionate

I seemed less blind- would I had felt the urge

To hasten to thee, for that signified

If weakness still –also- acknowledgement

The soul had yet a will, consideration

Might yet undo desires so blind, therefore

The haste to seize the pleasure ere the spirit

Reverted. For the first, the second time

Suspicion of the spirit then, bade haste.

Now I had no suspicion, fear of strength

More potent than the force which made a way

Magnetic to me, from thee faded, that

I paused and knew forgetfulness not essential

When right fought wrong if wrong was Margaret

Right bore his arms in vain, no ardent tenet

Buckler of principle could now prevail

Against lust's slender dragon; For a moment

Truth was strong in me, at the stairway's foot

That wound to thee, then as the interior

Grew clearer, my eyes functioned, the light

Without came through, the light within lost strength

The worlds flashed slowly over me; the moon

Drooped her grey folds about her kneeling limits

And sighed when sighed the wind; there was no moon

All night, nor any star feathered it's way,

But had its aimless gleam in the cold air.

No stone was lit up on the parapet

Wont to glow in the evening yellow moon

Or clasp the stars beneath a skim of rain

Earth in a dreadful hush lay wakefully

For all the winds, save one, were spent

This he stoked with his grey hands on the walls

And breathed, and crushed his mighty body close.

I faced thee backward, awkward, not as if

To yield conflicted with thy character

But as that character were worn and awkward

In this wise, crimson blooms filed up the walls

When fell icy tresses crusting on the slain

Amongst the many stairs of sandstone, there

Sparkling in places on the granite grey

Laying my face upon thy hair, to stay.

It's curling, for it's former smoothness was

A waiting uneasiness, and it uncoiled now

Taking the smiling and lascivious

Promise with it, like the heavy heart

I sent you, as I leaned forth and kissed you

C: Earth and Water

I touched your silken hair, satin it felt.

Then the blind, underground beasts when in silk

They hush their burrows warm as to the heat

Through famished red earth they rise and have

The moisture gleam along their deep waist-coats

Moving past the golden tendrils then my gaze

Came sudden against wall and mounting

In the poignant- short gloom became height piercing

Vague, vaguer as it paused on the thick sill

Cloudy- I sensed the cloud surge like a mood

Rose on, then all was gone the cerulean

Glowed everywhere, when without falling, soil

Poured in upon me like a dry cascade

Upon my bosom; and it found the water

Beneath, and blanched with cold and tremored me

The water sluiced to the right over bodies burned

Fondly in a slanted sheen so fine

Collusion of one element with the splashes

Left by the childish currents on the bulrush

And on the green ranks seemed abound.

I smiled.

If you are a dream, it is a mundane dream

The soil smells of you and your innocence,

World-glorified negation, of the earth

O God of Heaven, I have felt thine earth

And wondered at the kingdom in my hand

And I have smelled the mould, mad in its thrill

Have even rent one secret from its stubbornness-

For I smelled life therein, life in thee

Life of the warm life in a woman's hair

Tantalizing, pungent in the dark

A female odour, never feminine

The round stones soldered deeply in the path

How hard they are to loosen! This is thee-

In all my humanness; and lights shining

Brilliant in the afternoon in distant streets

After rain has come and lasted and gone

Another fragrant fragment of your being

Yet you were never perfumed, we left that to the flowers.

Your brow was animal, as was your hair

And the winds' hands at night are emotional

Like your two hands trembling on the grass.

The Bell *[probably intended as part of 'The Tower']*

As if a quietness now were descending

The sounds of day grow dimmer mingling more

And falling nearer to the earth, day's ending

Is not yet; and my soul will go before

There will not be the grey pall for my soul

I wished she were not going out with evening

Therefore these plain lines must take evening's role,

It swathes me and I die my virtues leaving

The wickedness I mourn comes bubbling through

And rise and I rise with them; if the bell

Struck three then let me go or I will rue

A passing at an hour I loved so well

For Margaret came at three- then no regret

The bell strikes three- I go to Margaret

The Raff

Riffraff is more like it. We weren't exactly the SAS anyway. I remember a big rough looking chap lying in the bunk above me crying for his Mam all night. (*Oh, Mam, I want me Mam!* Etc,) It was the first time a lot of us working-class lads (whose Dads had done all the *work* so far at any rate) had ever been away from home.

I had spent three weeks with my Auntie Janet in *Besses O'The Barn* – oh, and I went pea-picking with the school just outside Ormskirk for a week once - and that was about the extent of my travels before I was "called up". This was 1945, and the war was basically over, yet on my paybook it said "For the duration of the present emergency" which might have meant *anything* at all. Our wartime 'glorious ally' the Soviet Union was suddenly beginning to look a lot shadier, and things could change quick.

I felt a bit like Robert Doughnut in the *Chateau Deef* ("How long have you been in here for?" "Thirty years...!")

There were some strange-looking people in my "intake flight" or whatever it was. There was a seven-foot Hertfordshire giant with a heavy moustache called Roy Dutch (no, not the moustache!) a leather jacket and a pair of striped trousers that seemed to go on and on like the ones they use to hide their stilts with at the circus. He couldn't wait to get into his "blues", but he really had the blues by the time he got a uniform big enough.

You saw him wandering in and out of the NAAFI in his striped trousers long after the rest of us were itching away in those rough pants that rubbed the inside of your legs raw.

And there was a kind of human hedgehog from somewhere in Dorset with thick prickle-like hair growing down to just above his eyes and as I saw later, down the middle of his back. He could only grunt as far as I could make out, and the others got a lot of amusement out of him especially at night, when everybody wished him good night in turn

"G'Night Bill!"

"Urkknigh"...

"G`Night, Bill"

"Urknigh"...

"G`night Bill..."

It wasn't until about the twentieth "G'Night Bill!" that it dawned on Bill that they were taking the mickey. Then came the reaction they were gleefully waiting for. Bill, practically foaming at the mouth, began to utter weird, (fortunately unrecognizable) animal shrieks and roars until the final "G'night Bill!" came from the end bed.

And there was a Tommy Trinder Junior with a long chin and a cockney accent, and Billy Kuttner, a rather effeminate Jewish lad who claimed, improbably, to be distantly related to Will Fyffe (of all people) and had put new lyrics to a current tune called *Teeko Teeko Tock*:

" And if you want some tropic excitement,

And you find that things are going rather flat,

Da da da da da dee,

Da da da dee da dee,

And you'll find me at the Golden Bowler Hat,!"

I think he claimed to have sold it to Billy Cotton or somebody, but I can't remember who.

But mainly, the intake seemed to come from north of the Tweed, and suddenly I found myself in a Nissen Hut with all these Scots – Bill McWilliam, Geordie Tennant, Bill Love, and a slimy chap with boiled eyes who had once been a corporal and for some obscure reason had rejoined, And there was Alan Crystal, Ronsonol, and of course Corporal Brooks, that scurvy looking lout. Don't get me started on Corporals!

Our teeth were so bad that the Raff dentist actually complimented me on mine just because I had only a few fillings and nothing that urgently needed whipping out.

We were measured for our blues by a schizoid tailor:

"Just raise your arms a little more, sir... *Do you usually put your hands in your pockets when you are being spoken to?*"

Food was a shock not worth elaborating on. Those *awful* NAAFI potatoes, soaking for days, and those perpetually dirty irons, the ones we *really* used to eat with as opposed to the *Duraglit*-tering ones laid out for inspection.

"*Jus', because he had no duraglit/*

Waitin' at the Guardroom, fu'kit."

(With Scots you couldnt tell whether it was the F-word or not.)

Other chants:

"RAF Padgate Warrington Lancs-

Wanna be an airman? No thanks.."

And of course, snippets of long-gone overheard conversation have endured. Discussing their girlfriends in the dark. Mainly lies, of course, but with the occasional flash of sincerity:

"Could you love Tex? I love the way she lifts up her leg when she farts, like a chap".

And the classic barrack room lights out joke, involving many voices:

"Not the whip! Anything but the whip! "

"*Anything?*"

"Quick ...the whip!"

This was in the long huts at Watton in Norfolk. Strangely, I had time to wander around the landscape here, and actually spent considerable amounts of time strolling along fields of sugar beets. Ate one once, raw, just out of curiosity. I could still taste it years later.

I remember befriending a seed salesman who played chess and drove me all over Norfolk with him. He just wanted someone to keep him awake, I suppose, and to play chess with. His wife was an actress, and he had a big black cat called Hansel and a dachshund called Gretel with pneumonia. I can picture it now, this sausage dog lying on the pot rack over the cooker, sniffing eucalyptus fumes from a steaming kettle.

The seed salesman used to beat me at chess. It never dawned on him that I only knew the *moves* and had no idea how you actually won. But even my sketchy knowledge was worth some good suppers, and I managed to keep up the pretence. They were nice people.

I think I remember best travelling home. The train journeys round London and up past Ely in train corridors overflowing with teacups, looking at the yellow patches of light from the milk train windows reflected in the snow, to another planet.

And here I suppose boyhood simply ended, and Darwen became just another place in a world full of places, many of which I was about to set forth and discover. Not only Padgate, but Tuebingen, Svendborg, Bergen, Trondheim. Places I'd never heard of, but places where I eventually would go and, perhaps, give to them a bit of Lancashire.

Untitled 6

Killing a fly with the left side of his mind

plucking a hair absently from a nostril, a worm

of tobacco from his lip, trying to find

words to put a world in, the right term

for the shape of a head, the sound of a flower, the look
of trees:

A rhythm describing ripples on a lake,

the epithet for death, a woman's eyes,

aching to make other people ache,

lurking to take his readers by surprise,

filling a cullender with seventeen seas:

Daft as a brush, the poet, staring out

of a cold and open window into the street,

outlines another dream, acts as a tout

for the absolute, cleans his o with a pin, counts feet,

and finally rhymes philosophies with fees.

..

And all the Rest

Memories jumbled together, not quite following a connected narrative:

Wonderful Old Lancashire names from my childhood; Skillikorn, Waddicor, Thexton, Eccles, Cowsell, Rostron, Riding, Eleonor Bellman, Daisy Cowsell, Dorothy Thornber, Freddie Cronshaw, Dorothy Kershaw the giant milkmaid, Herbert Aldcroft, Graham Seddon, Downer Lofthouse, Rhona Green, and Bunty Ward was a spaniel.

Ashtubs on the cobblestones in the back street. One of the earliest sounds I can remember was the deep rolling sound of those great wooden barrels, hooped with iron, being rolled skillfully down the back street by the ashtub men.

Children squeeze the last drop out of their environment - the broken "flags" in Johnny Wraith Broo, the dents in the old garage on The Top...

Those flagstones were all different, in colour, and in the contours of the cracks on them, the sizes and the grass growing between them. I saw it as a sort of symbolic code. If I could only read it, I would know the secret of life! I know now that that was absolutely true, but I also know that I was able to read it but not to communicate it - it cannot be communicated.

I, like all children, soaked myself in the enormous private symbolism of contingent facts, in the strangeness of the world I had been brought into, a strangeness far deeper and more striking than the cheapjack secondary grotesqueness of art. The short, harsh grass on the moors, the big blackish stones of the Tower and the gay colours of Park flowers; the suspicious turning of cows' heads.

We had a broken grate in the back yard and to stop kids lifting it up, Dad had put a 56-pound weight on it - a sort of big iron cube. It said 56 lb on the weight so I have always had a good idea how heavy 56 lb was.

Dad was born in Leeds in 1887, as the third surviving child of Richard Harrison Clayborough and Mary (Polly) Fox. Richard was a block printer, and moved about a bit, changing employer from somewhere in Leeds to *Sandersons* Wallpaper in London, and after that to *Potters* Wallpapers in Darwen. Hence Dad ended up spending a good portion of his childhood in Chiswick.

My Dad's mind generally went back to a strange Dickensian world of pawnbrokers and *Bums* (bailiffs). He had stories of workers *popping* their false teeth or tools over the weekend and redeeming them on Monday mornings. One even popped a sheep's head.

He told me about a family struggling to keep out a bailiff who had got the end of his wooden leg in the door jamb and kept moving it up and down while they sawed it off.

"Were it your family, Dad?"

"Aye, well, maybe it wor" he chuckled.

Then there was the terrifying tale of his Grandma banging the 'beer jug' down in front of one of them, and making them run down to the pub to have it filled. And how they'd 'go over' if they didn't jump to it!

"Aye, and sh'd go over't next!", my mother flared up.

Recollections of little boys kicking a rag ball at Kew, of him holding horses' heads outside London clubs and lighting people through the London fog. A link-boy, he'd been, a character from a different age even then. Wonderful army stories, too.

But he never told you *anything* about his family tree.

"What was your mother called before she were married? "

"Thad'll do!" he scowled.

It seems to be that his parents were never married, and that Mary (Polly) Fox was Richard's 'common-law' wife. I don't know if this was all *that* shameful, or maybe it was just too much bother to explain.

There was a time when my Dad - who once cleaned my little sister's teeth with *Panshine* - developed a sort of a mania for *varnishing* everything, especially the furniture (it got sticky in summer and when we had a good fire going) and shoes. We all used to go round with like cracks in our shoes, a sort of "crackle finish" except where the dust and fluff had stuck to the varnish. Protests from my mother were met with

"Ay, don't be so bloody soft.... Onnyway, they look a bloody sight better than they did..."

Dad's favourite toffee was Holland Toffee, a sort of caramel that stuck to yer false teeth. Whether that was good or bad, I'm not sure.

Coming from an ignorant working-class family, I thought teeth just fell out when you were about 25-30 because everybody of that age I knew, was wearing or looking forward to wearing, false ones.

Well anyway, you broke the plates of Holland toffee with a toffee-hammer.

All part of the fun. As mentioned before, you had to make your own, and there were any number of indoor games you could get up to while waiting for your toffee to be hammered. Like *Consequences*, where each player in turn added a bit to a long narrative that was read out at the end.

I remember the time we played *Consequences* with Teresa's pal Jean Bardsley ('Anna May Wong' - Jean had a "donkey fringe" as it was called, and so had Anna the actress.)

Instead of just making a silly story, hers were real attempts, e.g. "..and they lived on a houseboat with their one girl, Anna"

(*May Wong*, I thought).

"I tried to make it all follow..."

I had never imagined you could take consequences SERIOUSLY.

I was writing things like *Sloppy Dick met missis Crompton at the chip shop...*

That was in the new front room at No. 26, with firelight shining on the silverplated rose vases.

I always liked the brilliant light from a naked bulb, but of course we had to have a shade for respectability with fringes that threw strange shadows into the corners and on to your book. It was a Woolworth's shade and after a bit it got burnt in places. But what more did you want? We were happy with it. You could be unhappy with a gold one from *Harrods*.

Teresa's other mate Marjorie was sort of half-glamorous for me. She treated me like a grown-up, though, unfortunately, I wasn't one. I remember she had a crush on Ray Milland, but then, who didn't? He was nearly the tops. The tops was Tyrone Power. Not *the* Top, though. Who except me can see it now, covered with dandelions and butterflies?

Those were the days!

But then I remember the factory smoke and the stink of the streets round Belgrave Mills where my Dad worked dragging heavy machinery about with the help of a rather dim mustached chap called Tabby; the stench of strong chemicals coming up through the gratings - the wire netting.

One chap called "Come here, come here!" and then he threw a pint potful of cold tea at us through the wire netting, cackling with glee.

It might have been then I truly decided that I *wasn't* going to end up working there. *Not bloody likely*, to rephrase (and re-accent) Eliza Doolittle.

Most hard labour I ever did, was pea-picking during the war. Something about doing our bit, and arranged somehow by St. Mary's, yet we got paid for it.

Well, I don't know about *Strawberry Fields forever*, but after a couple of days picking peas wads in in the fields round Ormskirk (too near Liverpool for my liking) I felt as though I'd been doing it forever with brown-stained hands and backache filling big wicker hampers you could climb into and which it took two strong men to lift and empty, at two shillings a time.

It warn't much, mates, even then. One or two lads, destined for big things, made over a pound a day.

They were allowed to stand for Sunday Mass because they were too stiff to kneel down.

Larry made quite a packet, I don't know how, but like the Lord he moved in mysterious ways. It was just the way things were, he didn't seem half as stiff I was and I didn't take much brass home (I never proudly tipped up my wages to my mother, she told me to keep it) I only got two shillings a week taking morning and evening papers round for Mr. Giggleswick, but I expect they have a union now.

I remember at the time I was delivering papers (during the war, it was), I had a crush on a girl who lived on Manor Road called Eileen Holden. It never struck me that she could have been a *Sausage* Holden, i.e. related to *R.W. Holden's Sausages*. Eleanor and Margaret Hargreaves worked there. They always had bloody rags on their hands, there were bits of Hargreave fingers in most of Holden's sausages.

Joe Dillon, so I heard, was employed on leaving school at a coal mine pushing trucks up an incline with his head. It was a shaven head with puffy, slitlike eyes. He was a tough kid all right. I made him swear on the Bible History not to come past a line on the seat of the desk we shared, but how I managed that I can't remember; he could have killed and eaten me. There must have been some reason; maybe he *liked* me? No, nobody did (or could have) except our mother.

Certainly not Patton.

There was nothing fire-eating about the skinny, bespectacled Patton I have in mind, any more than there was anything fatherly. His nickname, Loll, suggests he was as ice-cold as a lollipop, but as far as I was concerned anyway, there was no sweetness involved. Loll was the maths teacher at St. Mary's, and a cold coming you had of it with him until you broke the ice; then you found a lot of bloody cold water underneath

The one kid in the class who got on well with him was a bucktoothed brown eyed violin player called Bert who was obviously destined to end up as a Jesuit priest himself. For some unaccountable reason I once found myself in Bert's home in Accrington, where the principal item on display was a vast signed and coloured photo of the current Pope.

The poor kid never had a chance. Everybody liked Bert even though it turned out to be short for Bertrand, not Albert.

I managed to break my leg the year I should have gone to the grammar school – as further education was then called, so at the little Catholic college where I eventually landed, they put me into the second year without a great deal more ado, when I could have done with a lot more ado. Whilst this worked out reasonably with subjects like geography and history it wasn't so reasonable with "continuity" subjects like languages (Latin and French), or in particular, mathematics where I'd have been weak anyway.

Father Joe, the second master and a flail of the Lord, sacrificed several lunch- breaks to give me extra keep-up French lessons in the staff room. Although my French has never got much beyond the "napoo" level, I'll always be grateful to him for my School Cert pass. (I remember "Cully" Culligan, coming out of the fateful exam room and asking what was the French for cabbage. "Chou" somebody told him. "I my gawd!" Cully groaned, " I wrote *la cabbage!*").

As regards mathematics, I stopped Father Loll in the corridor greatly daring to tell him I hadn't got my maths exercise book back. "What do you want it for?" he said, "It's no use to you.". Maybe he was right about my maths, at that, but I'm pretty sure I'm right about *him*.

The priest-teachers; Poice, Billy Fish, Joe, etc. I still have them all drawn on the inside back cover of my thick green physics book, which wasn't used much for anything else. Come to think of it, I passed the school certificate in physics. God must have wanted me to, for some reason of his own. Perhaps he just wanted to show them that the exam was too easy.

Among the jolly books prescribed for my school certificate were Siegfried Sassoon's *Memoirs of a Fox-Hunting Man* and George Meredith's *Evan Harrington* ('The Great Mel'- oh, what fun). I never read either of them, and doubt if anybody else did. Actually, the *Sherstow's Progress* series with their strong anti-military content might have been interesting reading if properly recommended- but none of our Marist teachers ever touched them.

Setbacks tripped me up but didn't stop me though. My Oxford wasn't *at all* like Evelyn Waughs'. It was exclusively spent at the lowest end of the scale. No Lord Sebastian Flyte, Brideshead or bloody teddy bears; just digs, scouse accents, and swotting. I won't dwell on these issues any longer, anyway. The years have passed. At the end of Arthur Clarke's/Stanley Kubrick's *Space Odyssey*, after coming through the "stargate" to the other end of the universe, the explorer finds himself in a room with an old man and his own memories.

After 30 years abroad, that is how I see my own childhood; I come back to it through a stargate and find my end in my beginning, and to be honest, I'd much rather round this off with a list of toffees:

Licorice spoons

Dolly mixtures

Licorice whirls

Spanish bootlaces

Spanish spoons

Spanish plugs

Humbugs

Caramels

Fry's "Five Boys" chocolate

Cadbury's milk choc

Bourneville

Terry's

Turnovers

Holland toffee "sticks to yer teeth"

"Some hopes"

Bassett's and Wilkinson's Allsorts

The End

The Escalator

Well, here we are
Long past the selling date
On the escalator
And we don't know whether
we've gone up or down
Or even moved at all!

Alleyball

Alleyball is played every 7 July in Sunny Bank Street with the Olympia entry and the steps up to Earth Road marking the goalposts. The ball is a compact mass of old *Daily Heralds* soaked in strong tea and bound with tatching ends. The players wear cloth caps padded with the old pages of a pocket bible, cricket belts with snake buckles round their moleskin trousers and union shirts without collars. *No clogs to be worn or crabs to be used on the occasion!*

Record attendance was in 1936, Silver Jubilee Year. 350 people, including the wining team (Dr Thomas Costello, Bella the insultress of policemen on point duty, Owd Sammy Taypot, Mr Greenhalgh (manager of the 'Follow the Crowds to the' Palladium Cinema) and Mr Forest who kept the old comics stall in the Market Hall (where Terence McHugh developed diphtheria after drinking a *Bovril* at Redman's stall, or so my mother argued).

First prize is a Wandering Cup in white metal topped with a small bronze figurine of a navvy carrying a shovel and smoking a briar nosetickler pipe. Legend (in rotten Latin): *Absque Labore Nihil*.

Champion Team: Stansfield Street United.

Compiled and edited by Stephen H. Clayborough.

Cover Illustration by Arthur Clayborough, enhanced by The Branch. 'Jubillee Tower Enterprises' logo by The Branch.

JUBILEE TOWER ENTERPRISES

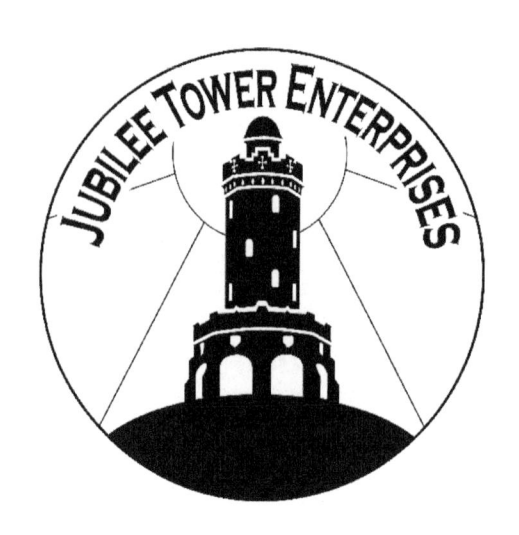

Printed in Great Britain
by Amazon